Washington

Byways

Twin Lakes Road (Tour 9)

Washington
Byways

56 of Washington's Best Adventure Roads

By Tony Huegel

WILDERNESS PRESS
BERKELEY, CA

Washington Byways

FIRST EDITION September 2003

Copyright © 2003 by Tony Huegel

Front cover photo © 2003 by Tony Huegel
Back cover photo © 2003 by Tony Huegel
Interior photos, except where noted, by Tony Huegel
Maps: Jerry Painter
Cover design: Larry B. Van Dyke
Book production: Margaret Copeland, Terragrafix, and Jaan Hitt
Book editor: Jessica Lage

ISBN 0-89997-299-3
UPC 7-19609-97299-0

Manufactured in the United States of America

Published by: **Wilderness Press**
                1200 5th Street
                Berkeley, CA 94710
                (800) 443-7227; FAX (510) 558-1696
                info@wildernesspress.com
                www.wildernesspress.com

Visit our website for a complete listing of our books and for ordering
information.

Cover photos: **Twin Lakes, tour 9** *(front);*
                   Kloshe Nanitch Lookout, tour 4 *(back)*
Frontispiece: **Twin Lakes Road, tour 9**

Disclaimer

Washington Byways has been prepared to help you enjoy backcountry driving. It assumes you will be driving a high-clearance four-wheel-drive vehicle that is properly equipped for backcountry travel on unpaved, sometimes unmaintained and primitive backcountry roads. It is not intended to be an exhaustive, all-encompassing authority on backcountry driving, nor is it intended to be your only source of information about the subject. There are risks and dangers that are inevitable when driving in the backcountry. The condition of backcountry roads can deteriorate quickly and substantially at any time. Thus, you may encounter road conditions considerably worse than what is described here. If you drive the roads listed in this book, or any other backcountry roads, you assume all risks, dangers and liability that may result from your actions. The author and the publisher of this book disclaim any and all liability for any injury, loss or damage that you, your passengers or your vehicle may incur.

Exercise the caution and good judgment that visiting the backcountry demands. Bring the proper supplies. Be prepared to deal with accidents, injuries, breakdowns and other problems yourself, because help will almost always be far away and a long time coming.

Guide To Trip Highlight Icons

Bird/Wildlife viewing	Photo opportunity	Hiking	Biking	Wildflowers
Camping	Lookout	Historic sites	Picnicking	Fishing
Boating		Dining		Caves

Map Key

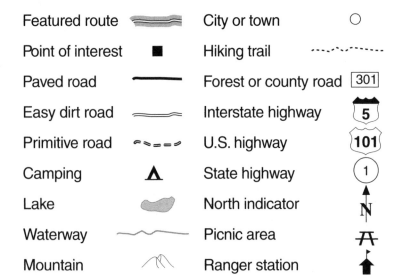

Featured route	City or town
Point of interest	Hiking trail
Paved road	Forest or county road 301
Easy dirt road	Interstate highway 5
Primitive road	U.S. highway 101
Camping A	State highway 1
Lake	North indicator N
Waterway	Picnic area
Mountain	Ranger station

Acknowledgments

Researching and writing *Washington Byways*, and the other books in my *Backcountry Byways* series, was made possible through the generosity, patience and endurance of many people. My wife, Lynn MacAusland, and our children, Hannah and Land, have made the countless miles memorable adventures indeed. Publicist Michael Dobrin, and Toyota Motor Sales, Inc., have been as unfailingly reliable and enduring in their support. The Toyotas that I use in my field research have covered thousands of punishing back-country miles without a single breakdown. Map designer Jerry Painter, as he has from the inception of the series, has again contributed his talent and skill. Paul Peck, who contributed the Long Beach Peninsula segment, and Mindy Chambers showed what friendship is about when my plans went awry on September 11, 2001. Finally, *Washington Byways*, like the other books in the series, has benefited from the work of the National Park Service, U.S. Forest Service and Bureau of Land Management. My thanks to you all.

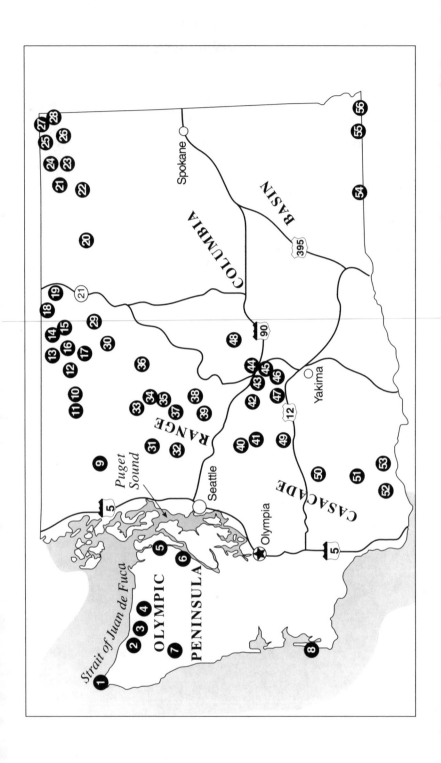

Contents

Appendix

Preface

Hiking, backpacking, mountain biking. . .when I was younger, fitter and more footloose, I enjoyed them all. But life always seems to make more, not fewer, demands on our time. Thus, over the years work, family and, I must admit, the passing of my physical prime took me away from those once-cherished modes of backcountry travel. As middle age appeared on the horizon, I worried that my days of wandering the wild were over.

Then I discovered that the American West's most beautiful and remote regions, occasionally even wilderness areas where mechanized travel is usually prohibited, are crossed by unpaved, often little-known roads. I learned that, with our factory-stock four-wheel-drive Toyota 4Runner, my family and I could have a wildland experience in the comfort of our family "car" anytime, whether for a few hours or a few days.

Bringing whatever amenities we wanted, we could explore rugged mountain ranges, high plateaus and remote desert canyons by day and then, if we didn't want to camp, relax at a motel at night. A child in diapers? We could carry a case of diapers. No time to hike? I could drive. That bothersome foot? It would never hold me back again. My kids' grandparents? Now they could come, too.

I'd broken free of the limitations of time, distance and physical ability. I'd learned that America's most beautiful wildlands were not just for the fit and free, the young and footloose, or those who drive motorcycles, ATVs and modified 4x4s. I found many unpaved roads to be easily driven, while many others were rough enough to provide substantial doses of adrenaline. I didn't need a winch, a lift kit, or oversized tires and wheels. Over the years, backcountry touring became an ever-bigger part of my family's outdoor life. With our children, their grandparents and our friends, we got to know the beauty and history of the American West in ways that would not have been possible for us otherwise.

Washington Byways, part of my series of backcountry touring guidebooks, will take you along many of the state's most beautiful and historic unpaved backways, which are among the most easily driven anywhere. You won't need a modified four-wheeler or monster SUV for these routes. In fact, most can be driven in today's car-based SUVs and light trucks, making wild Washington—from its rain forests and sagebrush steppes to its mountaintop lookouts and deep river canyons—accessible to a broad range of adventurous travelers. So why wait? All you have to do is turn the page, then hit the road.

Long Beach (Tour 8) ©*Paul Peck*

INTRODUCTION

Deer Park Road (Tour 3)

Coast to Canyons
Wandering Wild Washington

Although it is known by two simple nicknames—the Evergreen State and the Chinook State—the only state named for a president is a spectacular collision of many complex natural forces. You can liken its 71,300 square miles to a bag of Halloween candy. Reach in, and pull out a glacier or a volcano, a mossy rain forest or a sagebrush steppe, a moody beach or a forested archipelago, a river gorge or a Rocky Mountain vista, the sight of puffins bobbing in the Pacific surf or bighorn sheep grazing on a hillside.

More than 28 percent of Washington's land is publicly owned, not a great amount by the standards of the American West. (Neighboring Oregon is 52.4 percent public lands, and Idaho 61.6 percent.) Yet through it all is threaded one of the West's most extensive networks of relatively little-traveled, even little-known backcountry roads. A legacy of logging, mining, ranching, early-day settlement, even watching for wildfires from mountaintop lookouts, these roads are found in every corner of the state, every climate zone, every sort of terrain. For folks without the time, ability or inclination to hike—weekenders short on time, families with small children, disabled individuals, seniors, tourists just passing through—they are convenient and rewarding alternatives to hiking trails. Leave the asphalt behind, and you can experience a wilder side of Washington that is accessible in the comfort and convenience of any vehicle that is suited to exploring unpaved back roads.

Washington is ideally suited to this unique form of recreational driving. Its backcountry roads are quite good on the whole, and one would be hard-pressed to find anyplace on Earth with greater geographic diversity and natural beauty. It is the product of colliding continents, uplifted mountains, exploding volcanoes, vast lava flows, ocean air, ice-age glaciers, and catastrophic floods of biblical scale. Here one can stand on the northwesternmost point in the contiguous United States, Cape Flattery, home of the seafaring Makah Nation. Just 40 miles or so from the Pacific shore, in the rainiest place in the Lower 48, the uplifted Olympic Mountains soar to almost 8,000 feet, and are still capped by glaciers 10,000 years after the last ice age. Magical, temperate rain forests of Sitka spruce, western hemlock, soft mosses and tall ferns still stand here, protected by Olympic National Park and watered by average precipitation of 120 inches or more each year. Yet just outside the park, as you will see on some of the Olympic Peninsula trips in this book, clear cutting has devastated the ancient forests of Douglas fir, western hemlock and western red cedar. In their place now are what can only be described as densely planted timber farms, not diversified, living ecosystems. East of the Olympics, watercraft of every sort ply Puget Sound, a cluster of seawater-filled valleys dozed by glaciers. More than half the state's population is concentrated on the sound's eastern and southern shores, living atop hills of glacial debris.

Continuing east, one encounters the spine of the Cascade Range, which divides eastern and western Washington, and the dramatic, telltale cones of the Cascade volcanoes: Mt. Rainier, at 14,410 feet the state's highest point; Mt. Adams, 12,276; Mt. Baker, 10,800;

Glacier Peak, 10,539; and Mount St. Helens, just 8,363 feet now, having lost 1,314 feet in its huge 1980 eruption. The volcanoes remind us that the Earth remains restless in this meeting place of land and sea. According to the geologic theory of plate tectonics, far below the surface the oceanic Juan de Fuca Plate, a section of the Earth's crust, is moving east, and diving (subducting) beneath the westward-moving, continental North American Plate. As the Juan de Fuca Plate dives deep into the Earth's interior, the Olympics are being lifted. Heat and magma, being constantly generated, has vented now and then (in geologic time) through not just the Cascade volcanoes, but the fissures that formed the 180,000-square-mile Columbia Basin. Also called the Columbia Plateau, this desert-like region of volcanic basalt comprises two-thirds of eastern Washington, and extends into Oregon and Idaho as well.

Besides rolling hills of sagebrush and bunchgrasses, one finds in the Columbia Basin fertile soil, which, irrigated by the Columbia River system, is renowned for the apples, grapes and other edibles it produces. In the border country of southeastern Washington and southwestern Idaho—the Palouse—rolling, golden, dune-like hills are blanketed with wheat. But like the replanted timberlands of the west, they are an artificial, manicured and greatly altered monoculture, and what nature grew here isn't even a memory for most folks.

At Washington's far southeastern corner, where Washington, Idaho and Oregon meet, the waters of the Snake River spill out of Hells Canyon, North America's deepest gorge, on their way to the Columbia River and its gorge. The land has been deeply incised here by rivers and streams, creating countless canyons, ravines and narrow valleys. The Columbia in turn flows down from the Canadian Rockies to spill into the Pacific Ocean at Washington's far southwestern corner. But today's Columbia is far different from the wild river known to Native Americans for thousands of years, the one chronicled by Meriwether Lewis and William Clark 200 years ago. Of the 600 miles of river between the Bonneville Dam, east of Portland, Oregon, and the Canadian border, only about 50 miles can be termed free-flowing. The rest is impounded behind a series of massive hydropower dams. Gone is what William Clark described as "the horrid appearance of this agitated gut Swelling (water), boiling & whorling in every direction."

In contrast to Washington's well-watered western third, most of the less populated Columbia Basin is sagebrush steppe, dry and brown. Here in the rain shadow of the Cascades, which sap Pacific air currents of moisture, water is scarce. In contrast to the soggy ocean side of the Olympic Peninsula, where months can pass without a clear day, the sunnier Columbia Basin makes do with less than 10 inches of precipitation on average each year. Still, thanks to the Columbia and Snake rivers, the inland city of Lewiston, Idaho, about 465 miles from the ocean, is a seaport. At Hanford, on the banks of the Columbia, the World War II Manhattan Project found the water, power and isolation it needed to produce plutonium, although the ensuing half-century of nuclear-related work and waste left a costly legacy of radioactive contamination. The massive dams on the Columbia and Snake river systems house some of the world's greatest hydroelectric plants, to the detriment of the Northwest's decimated runs of migrating wild salmon. Dry as it is in the Columbia Basin, the thick volcanic basalt, which erupted from vents in the southeastern corner 13 million to 16 million years ago, has been incised not only by the Columbia and Snake rivers and their tributaries, but also by a series of ice-age deluges known as the Spokane floods, some 15,000 years ago.

While so much of the region east of the Cascade Range can't be described as "evergreen," the rumpled region along its border with British

Columbia, Canada, as well as the rugged northeastern corner, do look more like the Washington stereotype. Coastal air currents find their way here, bringing enough moisture to sustain a mix of coastal and Rocky Mountain vegetation. Rocky Mountain? Of all the images one may conjure up of Washington, among the least-likely might be that of a Rocky Mountain state. Yet its northeastern corner takes in a chunk of what's termed the Rocky Mountain Province, a tumultuous landscape of heavily glaciated uplands, steep-sided mountains and meandering river valleys. It stretches from the broad, undulating Okanogan Highlands east to the Selkirk Mountains, across the Idaho

©*Paul Peck*

Panhandle into Montana, and north into British Columbia. Here, one travels through mountains forested with ponderosa pine and Douglas fir, a dramatic contrast to the Columbia Basin's sagebrush hills, just to the south.

Much of the building, or assembling, of today's Washington began in the Rocky Mountain Province. It is thought that roughly 200 million years ago, as the supercontinent Pangaea broke up, what became North America moved west, and this area was the continent's western shore. As smaller microcontinents drifted east, they eventually collided with North America here in a geologic pileup. First to hit, perhaps 100 million years ago in the vicinity of the Columbia River valley, was the Okanogan microcontinent, which today is the glacier-scoured Okanogan Highlands of northeastern Washington and neighboring British Columbia. Some 50 million years ago, the eastern edge of the North Cascade microcontinent arrived in the vicinity of today's Okanogan Valley.

Descendants of people who braved the land bridge between northeastern Asia and northwestern North America occupied Washington for about 11,500 years before Spanish, English and American explorers began to probe the northwestern coast, in the late 1700s. West of the Cascades lived the Chinook, Makah, Quinalt and Salish people, among others. East of the range lived the Nez Perce, Yakama, Okanogan, Wenatchee and other tribes. British Captain George Vancouver did the first detailed survey of the coast and inland waters in 1792, and named many of its most famous features. After the United States acquired the region, part of the huge Louisiana Territory, from France in 1803, President Thomas Jefferson sent Lewis and Clark on their epic exploratory journey. The Corps Of Discovery floated down the Columbia River, the boundary between today's Washington and Oregon, and reached the Pacific Ocean in 1805. The first white settlers arrived in the 1830s through the 1850s. Congress created Washington Territory in 1853. Washington joined the union in 1889.

Almost six million people call Washington home now, the majority of them clustered along the shores of Puget Sound. The highways there are almost as congested as any in America, with Washingtonians commuting to all sorts of Pacific Rim livelihoods, from such high-tech and aerospace giants as Redmond's Microsoft and Seattle's Boeing to Bremerton's Puget Sound Naval Shipyard, the West Coast's largest. When their work is done, they know they are never far from the opportunity to venture where concrete and asphalt have yet to be poured. Rain forests, ice-age canyons, ghost towns, fjords, serene islands, snow-capped summits ... they have their pick. And so do you. Just reach into Washington's bag of wonders, pull out a treat and you're on your way.

How to Use
Washington Byways

LOCATION: Where the drive is.

HIGHLIGHTS: An overview of what I find to be the most appealing elements of the drive. (The icons accompanying each route suggest additional attractions, such as wildlife viewing, photo opportunities, hiking trails and campgrounds.)

DIFFICULTY: I assume that you are not a serious four-wheeler, but someone who drives a stock, high-clearance four-wheel-drive (4WD) vehicle that is suited to unpaved backcountry roads. The ratings I use, which are subjective but based on experience, are *easy, moderate* and *difficult. Easy* means it probably won't require 4WD unless conditions deteriorate. Most of the roads in *Washington Byways* fall into this category. Those that do are suitable to light-duty, all-weather SUVs and light trucks. *Moderate* means slower going in 4WD. Such roads may include rough spots, rocks, deep ruts and mud, but little or no technical terrain. They are best driven in a more heavy-duty vehicle that is equipped with a two-speed transfer case, all-terrain tires, and protective underbody "skid plates." *Difficult* means some technical four-wheeling, rough and slow going, and the possibility of vehicle damage. This sort of road typically requires a heavy-duty vehicle, and experience. Only one route, sandy Long Beach Peninsula (Tour 8), has the potential to fall into this category, depending on conditions. Remember, however, that storms, slides, floods and fires can alter conditions on any of these roads at any time, and can even close them altogether, without warning.

TIME & DISTANCE: The approximate time it will take to complete the drive (which can vary considerably, at your discretion), and the distance you will travel.

MAPS: Each route description is accompanied by an overview map. The route is highlighted. Scale is approximate. For route-finding, use at least one of the maps that I recommend here. In most cases, I recommend U.S. Forest Service maps. They are available at any ranger station, and many outdoor recreation equipment retailers, such as R.E.I. I also recommend the widely available *Washington Road & Recreation Atlas*. In each case, I cite the coordinates on each map where you'll find the route. Now and then I also suggest a supplementary flyer or brochure that might be useful.

INFORMATION: A source for road conditions and other information. Telephone numbers, addresses and Web sites (current at the time of publication) are listed in the back of the book.

GETTING THERE: How to reach the starting point. I typically describe routes going in a particular direction to help you locate landmarks, important turns and such. Many drives can be taken in the opposite direction.

REST STOPS: Picnic areas, campgrounds, historic sites and such that you'll find along the way.

THE DRIVE: Here I provide the details of the drive, such as directions, points of interest and historical background.

Author's Favorites

Tours 2, 3 & 7: Few of America's national parks rival the range of features found in Olympic National Park, which stretches from the Pacific Ocean across temperate inland rain forests to glacier-capped mountain summits. These three drives—Obstruction Point Road, Deer Park Road and Queets River Road, respectively—allow travelers to view them all. They also provide opportunities to hike and camp as well as sight-see among some of North America's unique and spectacular natural environments.

Tour 9: Twin Lakes Road, which is flanked by the majesty of Mt. Baker Wilderness, provides the opportunity to drive to a subalpine setting complete with two pretty lakes. The views of Mt. Baker and the surrounding glaciated landscape are inspiring indeed, as is the hike to historic, 6,521-foot-high Winchester Mountain Lookout. This one's another opportunity to blend an adventurous drive with world-class scenery and hiking.

Tours 10 & 11: The roads to Harts Pass and Slate Peak (the highest road in Washington) and down into the canyon of Slate Creek—all in the vicinity of the beautiful Methow Valley and North Cascades National Park—are not to be missed. They offer not only stunning alpine scenery, but plenty of opportunities for hiking, camping and mountain biking as well.

Tour 29: Ruby Loop winds through the foothills east of the Cascades, through a historic mining area complete with old town sites, mining roads and mines. The drier climate and more varied vegetation here in the rain shadow of the Cascades contrast with what one finds in the wetter, heavily forested western side of the state, and are reminiscent of the Rocky Mountains and Sierra Nevada.

Tour 34: Stormy Mountain Road climbs high into the steep and deeply furrowed Chelan Mountains, between the Entiat River and that great, water-filled glacial trough, Lake Chelan. The scenery is terrific, stretching from the Cascades to the Columbia Basin. If driving along the crest of high, meandering ridges and on narrow, exhilarating canyonside roads is appealing—and it should be—don't pass up this one.

Tour 56: Washington is far more than rainy conifer forests and endless irrigated farmlands. In the southeastern corner, it also has the narrow, deeply incised and terraced main and tributary canyons of the Snake River, which culminate in Hells Canyon, North America's deepest river gorge. While you can't drive into Hells Canyon, which forms the border between Oregon and Idaho, this trip will take you along the canyons of the Snake River and then high onto the benchlands above Hells Canyon. It continues into the beautiful, rolling mountains of northeastern Oregon.

Backcountry Touring 101
Rain Forests To River Canyons

Washington Byways will help you explore some of the state's most beautiful, remote and relatively wild places via unpaved back roads, hopefully in a vehicle—such as a sport-utility vehicle or pickup truck—that is suited to a wide range of terrain. In these pages you'll find descriptions of everything from manicured gravel roads to active logging roads and old wagon and mining roads. But road quality isn't the point. The point is that these roads will take you to places you might not have thought to visit before, perhaps because you've not known about them, how to find them, or what you'd be getting into. Backcountry touring, after all, isn't like highway travel, just as hiking isn't like walking a suburban greenbelt. There are things to know.

This isn't a guide to four-wheel-drive trails. You won't need a Hummer or a modified 4x4. In fact, many of the roads I describe are well-suited to today's less rugged car-based SUVs, even those without four-wheel drive. Most of the time, when conditions are good, having four-wheel drive, high ground clearance and all-terrain tires will simply help you travel with confidence, and without mishap. The point of backcountry touring isn't to pit your machine against nature, after all, but to explore rural and even wild areas conveniently, comfortably, responsibly and safely, free of the usual constraints of time, age, physical ability, even parental status.

When wandering the wild far from help, even on maintained back roads, one does need to be prepared for the unexpected. While most of the roads I take you on will be quite easy to drive when conditions are good, conditions can and will deteriorate rapidly and without warning. Storms, floods, fires, landslides and such can quickly damage or close any road in this book. Wildfires strip mountain slopes of vegetation, leading to slides, ruts and washouts. Fallen trees can block the way. Mud can turn out to be deeper than you thought. And in addition to nature's unpredictable impact, don't be surprised if you get two flats in a single day, leaving you without a spare. There will be times when you'll suddenly find yourself grill-to-grill with a fellow explorer who's going in the opposite direction on the same narrow mountainside road, with little room to pass. And out here, where road signs typically don't last very long, you'll cover many miles looking for the inevitable missed turns.

This is a uniquely rewarding form of recreational driving, yet problems are not just possible, but likely if you do a lot of it. And since relatively few people have substantial off-highway driving experience, I'm going to assume that yours is limited, and provide some basic know-how. Hopefully, these tips will help you have a safe and enjoyable experience while protecting Washington's natural environment, and historic and cultural sites.

KNOW YOUR VEHICLE. Some automakers, eager to tap into the motoring public's yen for at least the visage of ruggedness, apply the label "sport-utility" to just about anything with wheels. Don't be fooled. Know what you're driving, and drive within the vehicle's limits as well as your own.

NOT RECOMMENDED

Familiarize yourself with your four-wheel-drive system. Is it a full-time, a part-time or an automatic system? In a full-time, or permanent, 4WD system, all four wheels are continuously engaged as driving wheels; there is no 2WD mode. (A multi-mode system, however, will include a 2WD mode.) Full-time 4WD uses either a center differential or viscous coupling to allow the front and rear axles to turn independently for typical daily driving. Some systems will "lock" the center differential so that, in poor conditions, both axles will turn together for greater traction. A part-time system uses only the rear wheels as driving wheels until the driver engages 4WD. On pavement it must be disengaged from 4WD to avoid excessive drive train stress. An automatic system will sense on its own when 4WD should be engaged. All-wheel-drive (AWD) systems, such as those being used now in many passenger cars and vans, provide power to all four wheels much as full-time 4WD systems do. But AWD systems, and the vehicles equipped with them, are usually intended for all-weather use, not all-terrain use.

Does your vehicle have a transfer case? More than any other single feature, a transfer case identifies a vehicle that is particularly suited to all-terrain travel. It sends power to the front axles as well as to the rear axles, and, acting as an auxiliary transmission, provides a wider range of gear ratios for a wider range of conditions. It has three modes: high-range 2WD, high-range 4WD, and low-range 4WD. Use high-range 2WD for everyday driving in normal conditions, both on pavement and off. Use high-range 4WD when added traction is helpful or necessary on loose or slick surfaces, but when conditions are not difficult. Use low-range 4WD in difficult low-speed conditions when maximum traction and power are needed, and to keep engine revs high while moving slowly through rough or steep terrain.

Does your vehicle have all-season highway tires or all-terrain tires? Tires take a terrible beating in off-highway conditions, for which the latter are designed.

Does the vehicle have steel "skid plates" protecting undercarriage components like the oil pan, transfer case and transmission? Skid plates are essential to avoiding the damage that obstacles, particularly roadbed rocks, can inflict.

KNOW WHERE YOU'RE GOING. The maps in this book, while fairly detailed, are general overview maps. For route-finding, bring a statewide or regional map in addition to at least one detailed map illustrating the specific area you will be visiting and the roads you'll be driving.

For detail and navigational purposes, I usually recommend U.S. Forest Service maps, when applicable. They're informative, affordable, and foldable, contain lots of information, and cover large regions, including areas outside national forests. You'll need only a few of them to cover most of the routes in *Washington Byways*. U.S. Geological Survey topographic maps are good if you want greater detail, and the Washington State Department of Natural Resources produces maps for state forests as well. Commercial mapmakers who produce useful products include Benchmark Maps (*Washington Road & Recreation Atlas*), DeLorme (*Washington Atlas & Gazetteer*), and National Geographic/Trails Illustrated Maps. Increasingly popular are CD-ROMs containing topographic maps. While expensive, these programs can mark routes and pinpoint places of interest using Global Positioning System coordinates. Then you can print the maps (on special tear-resistant paper, if you wish), and bring them along.

Go over your maps before you set out. Become familiar with sights and landmarks to watch for along the way. As you travel, keep track of your progress so you don't miss important turnoffs, places of interest or worthwhile side trips.

Don't expect to find road signs. The Forest Service, in particular, does try to keep roads posted, but it's in a constant battle with vandals. So pay close attention to your maps and mileages. If you reach a junction where there are several routes to choose from and none has a sign, it's usually best to follow what appears to be the most heavily used route.

Global Positioning System (GPS) navigation units are increasingly popular. I'm sure some backcountry travelers find them handy at times, especially when trying to locate a hard-to-find point of interest, but I've not yet found them necessary.

When venturing into unfamiliar territory, it's sometimes best to rely on road numbers rather than road names, because rural and backcountry roads can have more than one name, or variations of the same name. However, you may find that roads can have more than one numerical designation as well. A county, for example, may use a number different from that assigned by the Forest Service.

Small spurs branch off most of the roads detailed in *Washington Byways*. Many are only obscure little two-tracks, and many have been closed to motorized use. Look for signs denoting their status. Open roads are usually marked with sign posts bearing green dots. Closed roads usually are posted with signs stating "no motor vehicles." But roads that are closed to motor vehicles often remain open to mountain bikes and hikers.

WEATHER AND WHEN TO GO. Because the state's boundaries encompass great geographic diversity, *Washington Byways* will take you through a broad range of climates and terrain, from sea level at Long Beach to over 7,000 feet in the North Cascades; from the cool darkness of an Olympic rain forest to the sunny warmth of a Columbia Basin sagebrush steppe; and from the broad benchlands above Hells Canyon to the valleys and peaks of the Northern Rocky Mountains. You will sample, sometimes close-up and sometimes from a distance, foggy beaches and old-growth forests, alpine lakes and sagebrush hills, long glacial valleys and narrow river canyons—and the wide-ranging weather that goes with them.

In a state with such a range of climate and terrain, you're bound to find somewhere to go in May through October. Fans of fall color will be lured into the wild in late September and October. Those who crave Washington's famous wild huckleberries face a varied summer season, but generally mid-to-late August is best. The state's infamous drizzly rainy season typically extends from October to July, depending on where you are. But its soggy reputation was made largely in the region west of the Cascades, particularly the Olympic Peninsula, one of the rainiest places on Earth. Low-lying areas of the southwestern peninsula average 120 inches of precipitation a year, for example (Mt. Olympus receives more than 220 inches, mostly as snow), with most of it falling in winter. In summer, typically a fairly dry season, daytime temperatures range from the mid-60s Fahrenheit into the 80s. As marine air moves inland across the mountains, it is sapped of moisture. So less than 30 miles northeast of Mt. Olympus the town of Sequim, which sits in the Olympics' so-called rain shadow, averages just 17 inches of precipitation a year. From there, eastbound air must cross the Cascade Range as well. By the time it reaches the Columbia Basin's Tri-Cities (Pasco, Richland and Kennewick), in the southeastern corner of the state, the skies have a scant seven inches of precipitation or less to give on average each year. So here, in defiance of the Evergreen State's image, trees are few, summertime temperatures often exceed 100 degrees, and although not technically a desert, the region is often referred to as such. To complicate matters further, there is the region that extends east from the Cascades along the Washington-Canada border to Idaho. Here, one encounters rolling, broad highlands, rugged and forested mountains, and a blend of coastal and Rocky Mountain climates and vegetation.

Some high-elevation roads, particularly in the North Cascades, can remain blocked by snow into June and July. July and August, when wildflowers bloom in the high parklands of the Cascades and Olympics, are Washington's driest months. Wild berries—including blackberries, blue elderberries, strawberries and much sought-after huckleberries—reward back-road explorers from mid-July through September, depending on location. Many consider September the best month overall, with its often-cloudless days, cooler nights, diminished crowds and hint of autumn. Autumn brings even cooler days and nights, colorful deciduous trees and bushes, bronzed grasslands, and warnings of winter, which arrives in November. Then comes the relentless drizzle, and the seemingly endless days of leaden skies.

Whenever you go, pay attention to the time of day. Don't set out on a long drive late in the day, because it's best not to risk being caught out there after dark unless you've planned an overnight stay. Pay attention to the sky, too, even the sky off in the distance, in case a storm is brewing. Stay out of narrow canyons if a storm seems likely, to avoid being caught in a flood. Dirt roads, when wet, can become slick and impassable, even with 4WD. Danger aside, driving on muddy roads leaves tracks that erode into ruts.

Since nature has a knack for rudely closing roads without considering our plans, it can be useful to stop at a visitor center or call ahead for the latest conditions. Unfortunately, though, finding out the latest road conditions can be difficult. Visitor centers and ranger stations are often staffed by volunteers who can help with campground locations and such, but who may not know backcountry roads well. To make matters worse, the most knowledgeable individuals at the agencies who manage public lands often are out in the field, not sitting by the telephone or at an information desk. So, spurred by the spirit of adventure, you may just have to check things out for yourself.

GOING ALONE. There is greater security in having more than one vehicle, and more than one source of ideas and labor if things go awry. It's also fun to be with other people. When you're on vacation, however, or venturing off for a few hours, a day or a weekend, you and yours will probably go alone, in a single vehicle. Now and then, too, an unexpected two-track going off to a canyon or mountain range will catch your eye, and you will succumb to its allure. That's OK, so long as your vehicle is reliable and you're prepared to handle emergencies alone. That said, during certain seasons, particularly summer, you may be surprised by how busy back roads can be, particularly those in the national parks. So while the more remote roads may provide genuine solitude, you may be sharing other roads with all sorts of users, from mountain bikers, hikers and equestrians to motorcyclists, ranchers and loggers.

RULES OF THE ROAD. Even in places where few other travelers are present, there are rules and practices to adhere to. The intent behind them is simple: to keep you and the people you'll encounter on the road safe, to keep your vehicle in good shape, and to protect and preserve wildlands and remote historic sites. Misconduct and mistakes can result in personal injury, damage to your vehicle, areas being closed, even legal penalties.

Here are some things to keep in mind:

• If your outing includes parking at a National Forest trailhead, you're likely to need a Northwest Forest Pass. These backcountry parking permits—priced at $5 for a day pass, $30 for an annual pass—can be purchased at any ranger station, and many retail businesses in Oregon and Washington.

Eighty percent of the revenue they generate goes to ecosystem restoration, new facilities and maintenance. They are mandatory at many locations, so you'll need to have one—or face a fine. Take it from me; this rule is enforced.

• Your vehicle must be street-legal to drive the routes in *Washington Byways*.

• Drive only on established roads where motor vehicles are permitted. Mechanized travel of any kind, including motorcycles and mountain bikes, is not allowed in designated wilderness areas and wilderness study areas unless a legal corridor exists. Never go "off-road," make a new route, or follow the tracks of someone who did.

• Watch for logging trucks. Washington has thousands of miles of active logging roads. Many are public roads, and are included here. Roads with logging traffic are usually well-posted as such. Often, too, you'll see painted on roadside rocks the CB radio channel that the truck drivers are using to communicate. If you bring a CB radio, you can tune into that channel and keep track of the trucks' whereabouts. You can also let the drivers know you're there, which can be important on single-lane roads where advance warning can help you find a safe place to pass.

• Avoid steep hillsides, stream banks and boggy areas.

• If you get lost or stuck, stay with your vehicle unless you are certain that help is nearby. A vehicle will be much easier for searchers to find than you will be if you've wandered off.

• Some of the places you will visit remain honeycombed with old, dangerous mines. View them from a distance.

• If you camp, use established campsites or areas that show previous use. Bring your own water (many campgrounds are waterless), and camp at least 300 feet from natural water sources to avoid pollution and to allow access by wildlife. Clean up the campsite before you leave, and take your trash with you.

• Leave gates as you find them, i.e., open or closed, unless a sign specifically instructs you to leave a gate open or closed. Don't disturb livestock.

• Don't drink directly from streams and springs.

• Don't park on grass, sagebrush and the like, because hot exhaust systems can start fires.

GO PREPARED. Things can go wrong out there, so be prepared to handle problems alone, perhaps even to spend a night or two. On the supplies side, the basics of backcountry driving are already on the packing list of experienced outdoors enthusiasts: maps, compass, extra eyeglasses and keys, binoculars, trash bags, matches, clothing for inclement weather, hats and sunscreen, blankets or sleeping bags, flashlights and batteries, food and water, and something that will make you easy to spot should someone have to come looking for you. Augment your supplies with enough non-perishable food and water for a couple of days in case you get stranded.

Here are some auto-oriented things to bring:

• Topped-off fuel tank. Fill up before every backcountry drive, every time. You will use your vehicle's low gears a lot, which will mean much higher fuel consumption than highway driving. It shouldn't be necessary to carry extra fuel. If you do, strap the container to the exterior of the vehicle, preferably the roof. Keep the container full so that dangerous fumes won't build up inside it.

• Shovel. Mine has been a lifesaver, and is the single most useful tool I carry.

• Traction aids. You're going to encounter poor conditions at some point, and sooner or later you're going to get stuck. Some people carry rolled up strips of heavy carpet, which are compact enough so that you can bring one for each tire for traction. They should be a few inches wider than your tires and about three feet long. Put holes in the ends, and when you use them, connect them with rope to the back of the vehicle. Then, when you drive off, they will follow, and you won't have to walk back to get them.

• Good tires. All-terrain tires are best. Even small bits of gravel, not to mention sharp volcanic rock, can easily puncture typical all-season passenger-car tires. Be sure you have a good (and properly inflated) spare tire, a jack, and a small board to support the jack on dirt. Also bring a couple of cans of pressurized tire sealant; a small electric air compressor (the kind that plugs into the cigarette lighter); and a tire-pressure gauge. A warning: Old mine sites are often littered with nails and broken glass.

• Some basic tools, including jumper cables, duct tape, electrical tape, baling wire, spare fuses, multipurpose knife, high-strength tow strap, small fire extinguisher, and a plastic sheet to put on the ground when making repairs. An assortment of screws, washers, nuts and such could come in handy as well, especially if you're driving an older or modified (meaning trouble-prone) vehicle.

I keep much of this stuff ready to go in a large plastic storage container. However you pack, tie it all down so it doesn't get tossed about.

Sometimes I bring my mountain bike as a backup vehicle. Since I do a lot of exploring, I also use it to check out places that I don't want to drive to. Consider getting a CB radio and roof antenna, even though transmitting range is limited. These days, a cellular telephone can be handy, although they often don't work in the wild.

OFF-HIGHWAY DRIVING. Most of the time, simply driving more slowly and cautiously than you do on paved roads will get you where you want to go and back again. Here are some tips for those inevitable times when the going will get rough.

All thumbs? You won't be for long if you forget to keep them on top of the steering wheel. Otherwise, the wheel's spokes can badly injure your thumbs if a front wheel is suddenly jerked in an unexpected direction. If the steering wheel is being rocked back and forth by the terrain, keep your hands loose on the wheel, at 10 and 2 o'clock.

Lean forward in rough conditions, keeping your back away from the seat, and you won't be tossed about so much.

Uphill traffic has the right of way, if practical, because it's usually easier and safer to back up to a pullout, using gravity as a brake, than to back down a slope while fighting the pull of gravity.

Think ahead. If you have a part-time 4WD system, engage it before you need it to stay out of trouble.

When in doubt, scout. If you're uncertain about the road ahead, check it out on foot..

Air down for sand, deep mud and rocky terrain. While standard tire pressure usually will provide adequate traction, deep mud and soft sand require temporarily airing down (letting air out) to 15 psi or perhaps even 10 psi to expand the tire's "footprint" for greater flotation. The risk in doing this, however, is that you will lose a bit of ground clearance and the tires' sidewalls will bulge, making them more vulnerable to cuts and punctures.

On rocky terrain, airing down to perhaps 20 psi will soften the ride and lessen the punishment the roadbed inflicts on you and the vehicle. On especially rocky and steep ground, airing down also will allow the tires to wrap themselves around the rocks for better grip. Shallow mud can be underlain by firm ground, so over-inflation can help tires penetrate to terra firma. Remember to return the tires to proper inflation (it's noted on the driver's side door-jamb sticker) before driving at speed or on pavement.

Maintain speed and forward momentum in mud and sand. Go as slow as you can, but as fast as you must. Slowing down or stopping in sand or mud can be the worst thing to do. Keep up your speed, and keep moving. Drive in established tracks, if possible. Higher gears tend to be more effective in poor-traction conditions than lower gears.

Because of the problems that driving in mud poses (roadbed damage, vehicle damage, transporting organisms from one ecosystem to another), avoid it. If a storm hits, you might want to pull onto firm ground and let it pass.

If you begin to lose traction in mud, turn the steering wheel rapidly one way and then the other, back and forth. That can help the tires grip. If you do get stuck, dig out the sides of the tires to relieve suction, and pack debris around the tires for traction.

Stick to the high points. When the going gets particularly rough, shift into low range, go slow, and keep the tires on the high places, thus keeping the undercarriage high and away from obstacles that can damage the differentials (so-called "pumpkins") or other components. Do not let large rocks pass directly beneath the vehicle.

Straddle ruts, letting them pass beneath the vehicle. If you must cross a rut, do so at an angle, easing one tire at a time across it. Do the same for depressions, dips, ledges or "steps," and ditches.

If you get stuck, don't panic. Calmly analyze the situation, and with thought and work, you'll get out. Don't spin your tires, which will dig you in deeper. What often helps is to jack up the vehicle and backfill the hole beneath the problem tire, perhaps building a base high enough to provide a rolling downhill start. Lower the vehicle, and if you're stuck in sand, lower the tire pressure to 10-15 psi to increase the tires' footprint.

If the vehicle gets high-centered, meaning your undercarriage is lodged on something and your tires can't grip the ground, take out your jack and the little board you brought to set it on. Carefully raise the vehicle, little by little, placing rocks, dirt and debris under each suspended tire until you've made a down-slope that will help you get going and keep going.

To get over a ledge, either use the rock ramp that is likely to be there already, or use a few nearby rocks to build one. (Don't leave an excavation site behind by taking lots of rocks from a single spot.) Put one wheel over the ledge at a time.

Be prepared to remove deadfall from the roadway, because occasionally, particularly in forested areas that have burned, you may encounter a fallen tree or limb in the road. It's usually possible to drive around it. If you must drive over it, approach at an angle and put one wheel at a time over it. If you carry a folding saw, as I do, cut it away. If the obstacle is too large to cut or move by hand, consider using your tow strap to pull it out of the way.

Have someone act as a spotter to help you maneuver through difficult places, and use low range and a low gear for better control.

Try not to spin your tires, which tears up the road and can get you stuck, or stuck worse than you already may be. Some newer 4WD vehicles have sophisticated electronic traction-control systems designed to eliminate wheel spin by instantly transferring power from spinning wheels to the wheel or wheels with traction. Some Toyota SUVs and trucks can be purchased with locking differentials, a.k.a. "lockers." These mechanisms vastly improve your ability to get through or out of nasty off-highway situations by equalizing power to the driving wheels and eliminating the differential's tendency to transfer power to the wheel with the least traction.

Uphill sections of road are often so badly chewed up by the spinning tires of vehicles that lack locking differentials or traction control systems that they resemble a ski hill's mogul run. If you encounter such a hill, shift into low range and keep your tires on the high spots between the holes.

Before climbing over a blind hilltop, find out what's on top and on the other side. Depending on how steep it is and how much power your vehicle has, shift into low range. Drive straight up, accelerate as you climb, keep moving, then slow down as you near the top.

If the engine stalls on a hill, immediately set the parking brake hard and tight. Here, an automatic transmission can help you get going again easily. Just shift into "park" and turn the key. If you have a manual transmission, you may be able to compression-start the engine if you're facing downhill. If you're facing uphill, try shifting into first gear/low range. Turn the engine over without clutching, and let the starter motor move things along until the engine starts and takes over. Otherwise, you'll have to work the clutch, hand brake and accelerator simultaneously to get going again without rolling backward. Modern clutch-equipped vehicles require the driver to depress the clutch pedal to start the engine, which is fine in a parking lot but difficult on a steep mountain incline. However, some vehicles have clutch bypass switches that let you start the engine without depressing the clutch, a great help when stalled on a climb.

If you can't make it up a hill, don't try to turn around. Stop, and put the transmission in reverse/low range. Tilt the exterior mirrors, if you can, so that you can see what the rear tires are doing. Then slowly back straight down. Never descend in neutral, relying on the brakes. If you must apply the brakes, do so lightly and steadily to minimize the risk of losing traction and going into a slide. Go straight down steep inclines, using low range and the lowest driving gear so the engine can help brake. But remember that automatic transmissions, which I think are best overall, don't provide as much engine-braking ability as manual transmissions.

Avoid traversing the side of a steep hill. Occasionally, though, mountain roads do cross steep slopes, sometimes tilting the vehicle "off-camber," or toward the downhill side. The fear of rolling makes this an unnerving experience indeed. Lean heavily (no pun intended) toward caution under such circumstances. You might want to remove cargo from the roof to lower your vehicle's already-high center of gravity. Then go slow. It might help to turn the front wheels a bit up-slope, into the hill. If you decide not to continue, do not attempt to turn around there. Tilt the exterior mirrors so you can watch the rear tires, shift into reverse/low range for greater low-speed control, and slowly back up until you reach a spot where you can turn around safely.

Don't cross waterways if there's an alternative. Fording streams and shallow rivers is fun, so long as that is the way the road goes (none in this book do). But many living things reside in or otherwise depend on streams, and can be harmed by careless and unnecessary crossings, which stir up sediment and erode stream banks. If you must cross, use an established crossing point. Check the depth with a stick if necessary, comparing the depth to your vehicle (hub deep generally is the deepest you should go). Or walk across first. Don't cross if the current is fast and deep. Never enter a desert wash if it's flooding. Often, a somewhat fast-moving perennial stream will be safer to cross than a sluggish one, because continuously moving water prevents sediments from settling, keeping the bed rocky and firm. Slow-moving or still water, on the other hand, lets sediment and mud build up.

Once across, stop and inspect the vehicle. The brakes will be wet, so use them a few times to dry them out. The tires also will be wet, and may not grip the roadbed as well.

ACCESSORIES AND SUCH. Many 4WD SUVs and pickups come from the factory ready to take people to places that sedans, vans and station wagons either cannot go, or shouldn't. Despite their comforts, many are rugged and reliable transport that can go from the showroom straight into the hills without modifications.

One of my family's two Toyota 4Runners has a 5-speed manual transmission and a stock 4-cylinder engine, which I've found to be adequate even when it's loaded with the four of us and our camping gear. The other has a V6 and automatic transmission. I've never felt any need for a thirsty, high-powered V8. You will find that at times manual transmissions require three feet: one for the brake, one for the clutch and one for the accelerator, all working pretty much simultaneously. So I prefer automatic transmissions, which are much easier to use in the rough.

I've learned to appreciate options that I once dismissed as unnecessary. Easily adjusted electric side mirrors, for example, will pay for themselves the first time you have to back up or down a narrow shelf road with a drop-off on one side and a cliff on the other. And when exploring narrow, high-walled canyons, a sunroof/moonroof is a handy option indeed.

There is a huge four-wheel-drive accessories market. Are those add-ons necessary? It depends on how much, and what type, of adventure motoring you plan to do. Stock vehicles will do fine on the routes in this book, which fall mostly into my "easy" category. The requirements of serious four-wheel-ing on technically challenging routes generally differ from those of back-country touring. The former can require extensive vehicle modifications, which can degrade on-highway performance and reliability. The latter does not. Still, if you enjoy traveling the West's more remote backcountry roads, you never know what you might encounter, so there can be real benefits to adding extra lights, beefier tires, a more versatile roof carrier, heavier skid plates, perhaps even an after-market locking differential. (In case you're wondering, I've never owned or needed a winch.)

Maintenance is essential. Backcountry roads are hard on vehicles, so fol-low the recommendations in your owner's manual for dusty, wet and muddy conditions, sometimes listed as "severe" use. Check the tires often, because no part of your vehicle will take a greater beating. If you pass through an old mining area, expect to pick up a nail.

FAMILY FUN. Backcountry roads provide terrific opportunities to explore wildlands easily and conveniently, but trying to keep kids happy on car trips has always been tough. Still, there are things you can do to make touring the backcountry fun for them.

• Don't just drive. Stop, and stop often. Watch for wildlife, especially early in the morning or evening. Visit historic and geologic sites, climb up a lookout tower, or take a hike.

• Pick up a book or two that will help you identify, understand and explain the region's history, scenery, vegetation and wildlife. Looking up the story behind place names can be fun as well.

• Make a photocopy of the area on the map that depicts where you'll be going. Let the kids help you navigate and identify peaks, creeks and other landmarks.

• Bring at least one personal cassette or CD player. If you have small children, check out some children's cassette tapes or CDs from your public library. They've been trip savers for my family on many long journeys. Audio books, which I listen to myself on long drives, are great diversions for children as well. Many video rental stores carry them.

• Bring an inexpensive point-and-shoot camera and binoculars for the kids to use.

• If you have a licensed teenage driver on board, let him or her drive now and then. The sooner a teen learns backcountry driving skills, the longer he or she will remain a participant. And someday you may need a capable co-pilot.

• Bring snacks and drinks. Plastic garbage bags, paper towels, changes of clothing, wet wipes and pillows are also good to have along.

PRESERVE THE PRIVILEGE. If you're particularly interested in helping to preserve opportunities to travel responsibly through public lands, contact Tread Lightly!, Inc., an Ogden, Utah-based non-profit organization founded to promote responsible use of off-highway vehicles.

As you travel, tell me what you've found, whether it's mistakes, or trips and tips you'd like to see added to future editions. You can write to me in care of Wilderness Press, 1200 5th St., Berkeley, CA 94710.

Queets River Road (Tour 7)

THE TOURS

Cape Flattery

LOCATION: Makah Indian Reservation, in the northwest corner of Washington where the Pacific and the Strait of Juan de Fuca meet.

HIGHLIGHTS: Cape Flattery, the most northwestern point in the contiguous states, is the home of the Makah Nation. It was named in 1778 by British Capt. James Cook for the point of land that "flattered us with the hopes of finding a harbour." You will take a short boardwalk hike through an enchanting forest to the lip of a cliff above the surf. From a platform, you can watch puffins bobbing on the waves, look out at the lighthouse on Tatoosh Island, perhaps see seals and whales in the distance—if the weather in this cool and rainy place cooperates (bring a jacket). In summer, free guided tours of the cape are provided Wednesday through Sunday at 3 p.m. Meet at the trailhead. **Note:** Visitors in motor vehicles must purchase a permit ($7), available at many Neah Bay businesses.

DIFFICULTY: Easy. The first 3.2 miles are paved. The remainder is well-maintained, low-clearance two-lane dirt and gravel. High clearance is advisable for the short, optional segment at the end that leads to a viewpoint.

TIME & DISTANCE: 1 hour; 16 miles round-trip. Add an hour for the 1.5-mile (round trip) boardwalk foot trail through the Makah Wilderness.

MAP: *Washington Road & Recreation Atlas*, p. 52 (A-B, 1-2).

INFORMATION: Makah Cultural and Research Center.

GETTING THERE: Take S.R. 112 west through Neah Bay to a T, where an Indian Health Services clinic will be on the right and a Presbyterian church on the left. Go right here, drive a block, then go left. Set your odometer to 0, and follow the signs for Cape Flattery Trail and the tribal center.

REST STOPS: Neah Bay has all services. The Makah Museum, in Neah Bay, is considered one of the country's best tribal museums.

THE DRIVE: About 2.5 miles from town, paved Arrowhead Road passes the Makah Tribal Center and the left (south) turn to a fish hatchery. The pavement ends a bit farther. Then you'll continue through a possibly foggy coastal forest. After 7.5 miles you'll reach the trailhead parking area. Park here, then follow the boardwalk trail through the Makah Wilderness, a verdant coastal rain forest that looks like something from a Tolkien fantasy. It ends at a platform from which you can gaze a half mile out at the old (1857) lighthouse on Tatoosh Island, which was the tip of the cape until the ocean eroded the land that connected it to today's cape. It was here that ancestors of the seafaring Makah—whale hunters and fishermen—first saw early European explorers. If the day is clear, from the parking area take the road's more rudimentary right fork for 0.6 mile to another viewpoint.

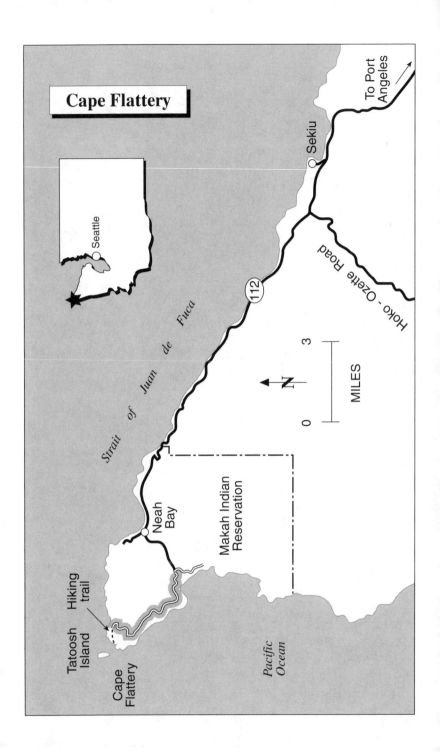

Cape Flattery

Seattle

Strait of Juan de Fuca

112

To Port Angeles

Sekiu

Hoko - Ozette Road

N

0 ——— 3

MILES

Neah Bay

Makah Indian Reservation

Hiking trail

Tatoosh Island

Cape Flattery

Pacific Ocean

Cape Flattery Trail (Tour 1)

Obstruction Point Road (Tour 2)

Obstruction Point Road

LOCATION: Olympic National Park. South of U.S. 101 and Port Angeles. Clallam County.

HIGHLIGHTS: With its wildflowers and views of the Olympic Mountains, particularly glacier-capped 7,965-foot Mt. Olympus and the park's deep river valleys, this short, narrow and winding ridgeline road packs a powerful scenic punch as it climbs to 6,150 feet. It runs both just below and on top of Hurricane Ridge (named for the winds that blow in winter), and ends above tree line at the base of 6,450-foot Obstruction Peak. The parking area at the end of the road is the trailhead for a number of day hikes, including the steep, 7.6-mile (one way) Grand Ridge Trail to Deer Park (Tour 3).

DIFFICULTY: Easy, on a good high-clearance, native-surface road. The park tries to have the road open by July 4, depending on weather and the previous winter's snowpack. It is generally closed to overnight parking in early October. It is closed altogether by the end of October. It is also closed whenever snow, which can occur anytime, makes driving hazardous. This is a busy road on sunny summer weekends, and the parking area at the end fills up fast. So consider going on a weekday if you can, or going early in the day.

TIME & DISTANCE: 1 hour; 15.6 miles round-trip. But this is a great day-hiking and sightseeing destination, so plan on spending considerably more time.

MAPS: The map you'll receive upon entering the park (and paying the $10 fee) is adequate. It is also shown in *Washington Road & Recreation Atlas*, p. 54 (E-G, 3-4).

INFORMATION: Olympic National Park.

GETTING THERE: From Port Angeles, take South Race Street southeast to Mt. Angeles Road, which will take you to Heart O' the Hills Road and the park entrance ($10). Follow Heart O' the Hills Road to Hurricane Ridge Visitor Center. Just before you reach the visitor center, look for a small sign for Obstruction Point Road, on the left. It's easy to miss. Set your odometer to 0.

REST STOPS: Heart O' the Hills Campground, near the park entrance. Hurricane Ridge Visitor Center and picnic area.

THE DRIVE: The little road, a mere shelf at first on the south-facing wall of Hurricane Ridge, immediately drops below the ridge. On your right is the plunging canyon of the Lillian River. The road takes you through a bit of sub-alpine forest at first, then crosses the ridge. In just a mile and half or so you will have some of the country's most impressive coastal mountains spread out before you, with their shimmering glaciers, snowfields and steep-walled river valleys. For safety, stop to take in the view, and be aware of other vehicles. Soon the road brings you to the top of the ridge, where you will meander through sky-scraping meadows splashed with wildflowers. In short order, unfortunately, you will reach road's

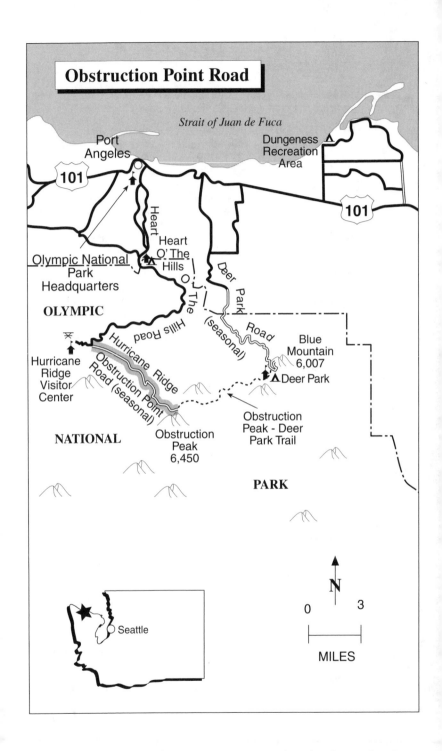

Obstruction Point Road

Strait of Juan de Fuca

Port Angeles

Dungeness Recreation Area

101

Heart

Heart O' The Hills

Olympic National Park Headquarters

OLYMPIC

Deer Park Road (seasonal)

O' The Hills Road

Hurricane Ridge

Blue Mountain 6,007

Deer Park

Hurricane Ridge Visitor Center

Obstruction Point Road (seasonal)

Obstruction Peak - Deer Park Trail

NATIONAL

Obstruction Peak 6,450

PARK

N

0   3

Seattle

MILES

end. If there's room to park, you can savor a sweeping vista that reaches from Mt. Olympus' glaciers to ships plying the waters of the Strait of Juan de Fuca, less than 20 miles to the north.

25

Deer Park Road

LOCATION: Olympic National Park. South of U.S. 101 and southeast of Port Angeles. Clallam County.

HIGHLIGHTS: This exhilarating drive climbs from 200 feet or so above sea level to a mile-high ridge. It ends at a vista point and hiking trailhead on 6,007-ft. Blue Mountain, north of the meadow for which the road is named. Weather permitting (it's generally drier here than the area of Hurricane Ridge/Obstruction Point Road, Tour 2), the views can extend from the park's glacier-carved Olympic peaks, sub-alpine tundra and deep river valleys, across the Strait of Juan de Fuca to Vancouver Island and Puget Sound to Mt. Baker. A 7.6-mile hiking trail connects Deer Park with Obstruction Peak and Obstruction Point Road.

DIFFICULTY: Easy, on a good high-clearance, native-surface road. The first 8.6 miles are paved. The remainder is narrow, steep and serpentine, with blind curves. This road generally receives less snow than Obstruction Point Road, so it can have a longer driving season. It is often open by mid- to late-June, sometimes even earlier depending on the area's variable weather and the previous winter's snowpack. The road is closed to vehicles 2.5 miles below the campground by early October, with weather determining the overall seasonal closure. Call ahead.

TIME & DISTANCE: 1.5 hours; 34 miles round-trip. But it's a prime venue for camping, hiking, wildflower photography and picnicking, so plan to spend a day or weekend.

MAPS: The map that visitors receive upon paying the $10 entrance fee is adequate. The route is also shown in *Washington Road & Recreation Atlas*, p. 54 (G, 2-3).

INFORMATION: Olympic National Park. There is a ranger station near the campground, not far from the end of the road.

GETTING THERE: Take U.S. 101 east from Port Angeles to milepost 253. Deer Park Road heads south from the highway where U.S. 101 makes a long southward U. Set your odometer to 0 there.

REST STOPS: Deer Park Campground, near road's end.

THE DRIVE: Follow the two-lane road directly toward the mountains and into the park. Beyond pavement's end, the road climbs steadily through forest and past road banks lush with moss and ferns. Soon views of the interior Olympics, namesake of the peninsula as well as the park, begin to emerge—steep river valleys, long ridgelines, virgin forests and snowy, craggy peaks. By about mile 15 the road narrows to a shelf, followed by a traverse across a steep, open slope that provides an unfettered view (on a clear day) of Vancouver Island. A short distance later you will have a bird's-eye view of the craggy, snow-and-ice-capped Olympic Mountains. The campground and ranger station are just beyond. Continue climbing to road's end, at a viewpoint about 5,600 feet above sea level. From the parking area you can take the

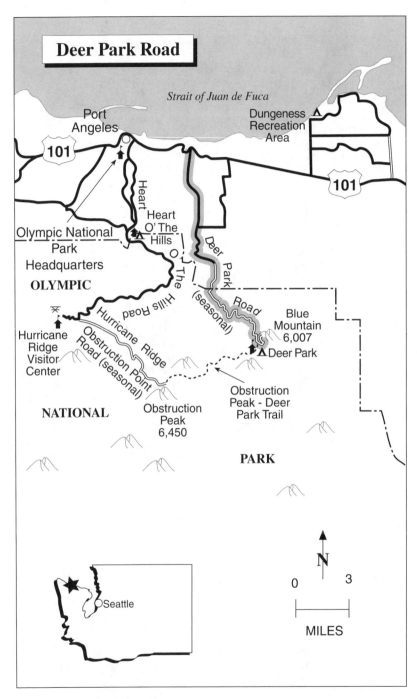

Deer Park Road

Strait of Juan de Fuca

Port Angeles

Dungeness Recreation Area

101

101

Heart O' The Hills

Heart O' The Hills

Olympic National Park Headquarters

OLYMPIC

Deer Park Road (seasonal)

Blue Mountain 6,007

Hurricane Ridge Visitor Center

Hurricane Ridge Road

Hills Road

Obstruction Point Road (seasonal)

Deer Park

NATIONAL

Obstruction Peak - Deer Park Trail

Obstruction Peak 6,450

PARK

N

0   3

MILES

Seattle

half-mile Rain Shadow Trail, a loop around Blue Mountain that is named for its location in the less-wet rain shadow of the Olympics.

Deer Park Road (Tour 3)

Kloshe Nanitch Lookout (Tour 4)

Pyramid Mtn.-Kloshe Nanitch

LOCATION: Olympic Peninsula. Olympic National Forest, near the northwest corner of Olympic National Park. Clallam County.

HIGHLIGHTS: You'll drive to the edge of old-growth forest while enjoying vistas across the Strait of Juan de Fuca to Vancouver Island. You can experience the old-growth forest afoot on the ridgeline hike to a shack that was a World War II aircraft spotting station, atop 3,000-foot Pyramid Mountain (a.k.a. Pyramid Peak). Picturesque Kloshe Nanitch is a replica of a fire lookout built about 1916-1917 on the brink of a cliff. It provides a magnificent view of the Olympic Mountains and Sol Duc Valley. The original lookout was destroyed in an explosion. The replacement was later moved to North Point, just beyond Kloshe Nanitch. It's now part of an electronics site.

DIFFICULTY: Easy. Narrow with blind curves. The 7 miles between Kloshe Nanitch and the Forest Service's Snider Work Station are steep, loose and rough, and will require a high-clearance vehicle. The hike to Pyramid Mountain is moderately strenuous.

TIME & DISTANCE: About 4.5 hours and 44 miles, including the one-hour, 1.25-mile (round-trip) hike to Pyramid Mountain.

MAPS: Olympic National Forest & National Park (E-H, 3-4). *Washington Road & Recreation Atlas*, pp. 52-53 (D-E, 6-9).

INFORMATION: O.N.F.'s Pacific Ranger District, Forks Office.

GETTING THERE: From the northeast (the way I describe): Take S.R. 112 to East Twin River Road (3040), 8.2 miles west of Joyce. Set your odometer to 0 and follow 3040. **From the south**: Take U.S. 101 to West Snider Road (8.5 miles west of Lake Crescent, 7.4 miles east of U.S. 101/S.R. 113). Take West Snider Road to Snider Work Station. Follow the signs for road 3040 and Kloshe Nanitch.

REST STOPS: Kloshe Nanitch has tables and a toilet, but no water. It may eventually be available for overnight rental; check with the Forest Service. Klahowya Campground is near Snider Work Station.

THE DRIVE: From S.R. 112, East Twin River Road (3040) winds below a beautiful forest canopy. Soon it narrows to a single lane as it meanders along the canyon of the East Twin River. About 7.2 miles from the highway is the junction with road 3068. Road 3040 continues ahead, to Kloshe Nanitch. You'll return to it. For now, go left (east), taking 3068 toward Pyramid Mountain. This road runs below a ridge that separates the logged and replanted national forest and the park, with its protected stands of old-growth alder and fir. At 9.7 miles from the junction, the trailhead for the hike up to Pyramid Mountain (the left branch) or down to Lake Crescent (the right branch) will be on your right. Park, and hike along the ridge past massive old firs, to an old

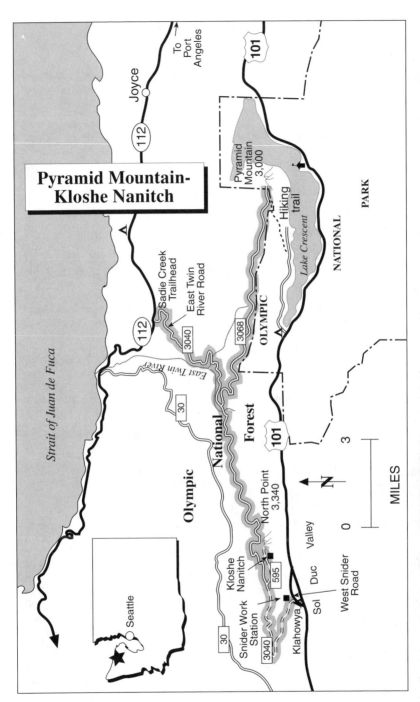

Pyramid Mountain-Kloshe Nanitch

shack above Lake Crescent. Return to road 3040, and follow it 8.2 miles to the turnoff (road 595) to the lookout. It's 1.4 miles to the lookout, on a rock outcrop overlooking Sol Duc Valley. From the lookout, follow narrow road 3040 down the south side of the ridge, and you'll come out at Snider Work Center and West Snider Road, which connects in a short distance with U.S. 101.

Bon Jon Pass

LOCATION: East side of the Olympic Peninsula, south of Sequim Bay and east of Olympic National Park. Olympic National Forest. Clallam and Jefferson counties.

HIGHLIGHTS: Although the route passes logged areas, it does wind among deep, forested valleys and high ridges that provide fabulous views of the Olympic Mountains and, in the distance to the east, the Cascade Range. Much of the route follows a U.S. Forest Service auto tour that explains the area's logging history, wildlife and vegetation at 10 stops.

DIFFICULTY: Easy, on a mix of asphalt, gravel and dirt.

TIME & DISTANCE: 3 hours; 40 miles.

MAPS: Olympic National Forest & National Park (P-Q, 5-6). *Washington Road & Recreation Atlas*, pp. 54-55 (E-H, 5-8), 68-69 (A-B, 6-7).

INFORMATION: Olympic National Forest's Hood Canal Ranger District, Quilcene Office, where you can borrow copies of the *Quilcene Auto Tour* interpretive booklet and cassette tape.

GETTING THERE: To go north (the way I describe it): A half-mile north of the U.S. 101 bridge over the Big Quilcene River, turn west onto paved Penny Creek Road and set your odometer to 0. **To go south:** About 2.5 miles southeast of Sequim, turn south off U.S. 101 onto Palo Alto Road.

REST STOPS: Dungeness Forks Campground. East Crossing Campground is closed due to a landslide.

THE DRIVE: Follow Penny Creek Road past a quarry and into the forest, driving in the shade cast by a canopy of tall trees. At 1.4 miles from U.S. 101 is a Y. Penny Creek Road is to the right, but continue ahead on Big Quilcene River Road (3057). Soon you will enter the national forest, where the road's number changes to 27 as it takes you south toward the river, then west and north around the Quilcene Range. Though the area has been logged, it has been replanted with a new crop. That fact, and glimpses of snowy Olympic peaks, help to impart a sense that you're still in the midst of a wildland. About 6 miles from U.S. 101 is a pullout with a view across the drainage of the Big Quilcene River and Buckhorn Wilderness to the park's majestic, glacier-carved peaks. Continuing north on road 27, you will see Mt. Baker and the Cascades looming to the northeast. Then the road descends to Deadfall Creek and the junction with road 28, which comes in from the right and continues ahead. Continue northwest on road 28, and you will soon see signs for stops along the Quilcene Auto Tour, which begins to the east at Lords Lake (via road 28). In 1.3 miles you'll be on Bon Jon Pass. Road 28 is closed by a slide north of the pass, so go right and take road 2810 past Mt. Zion. Follow 2810 until you rejoin road 28. Go right there, and take 28 to Palo Alto Road, which will take you to U.S. 101 in 7.8 miles.

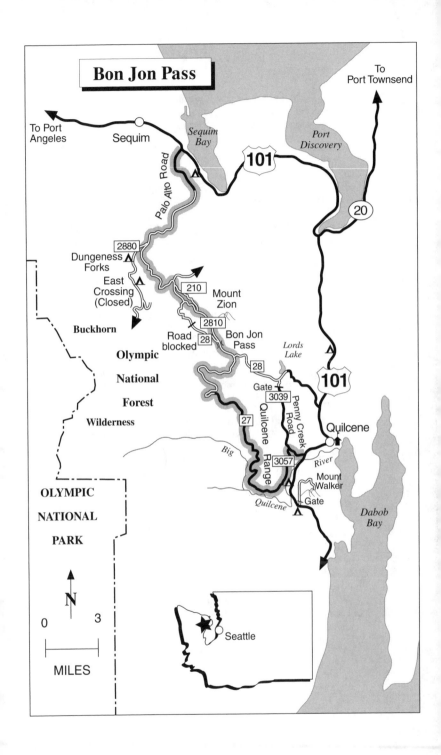

Mt. Walker

LOCATION: On the Olympic Peninsula, about 5 miles south of Quilcene between U.S. 101, and Dabob Bay and Quilcene Bay. Olympic National Forest. Jefferson County.

HIGHLIGHTS: Mt. Walker is the only peak facing Puget Sound that has a road to its summit. Once on its 2,804-foot summit, you will find broad vistas at the north and south viewpoints. The views stretch across the seawater-filled glacial valley called Hood Canal to Puget Sound, much of northwestern Washington, and to Canada. The views also take in the Olympic Mountains, Mt. Baker, Mt. Rainier, and the cities of Seattle, Tacoma and Everett. Native Pacific rhododendron grows along the road and at both viewpoints, blooming in May and June.

DIFFICULTY: Easy, on a maintained gravel road that is suitable for 2WD vehicles.

TIME & DISTANCE: 45 minutes; 9.5 miles round-trip.

MAPS: Olympic National Forest & National Park (P-Q, 5-6). *Washington Road & Recreation Atlas*, p. 69 (B, 7-8).

INFORMATION: Olympic National Forest's Hood Canal Ranger District North, Quilcene Office.

GETTING THERE: Take U.S. 101 along Hood Canal to Walker Pass, 5 miles south of Quilcene. Turn north onto road 2730. You'll see the sign for Mt. Walker. Set your odometer to 0 there.

REST STOPS: There are toilets at the viewpoints and tables at the north viewpoint. Neither site has water or camping, but Rainbow and Falls View campgrounds are on U.S. 101.

THE DRIVE: Single-lane road 2730—Mt. Walker Viewpoint Road—climbs from the northeast side of U.S. 101, ascending almost 2,000 feet through forest thick with century-old Douglas fir. At 4.3 miles from the highway you will come to a T-junction. The south viewpoint is to the right, the north viewpoint to the left. Each offers a unique birds-eye view across the heavily glaciated landscape of northwestern Washington, especially on a clear day. The views make Mt. Walker a popular destination, so expect to encounter other vehicles on its many twists and bends.

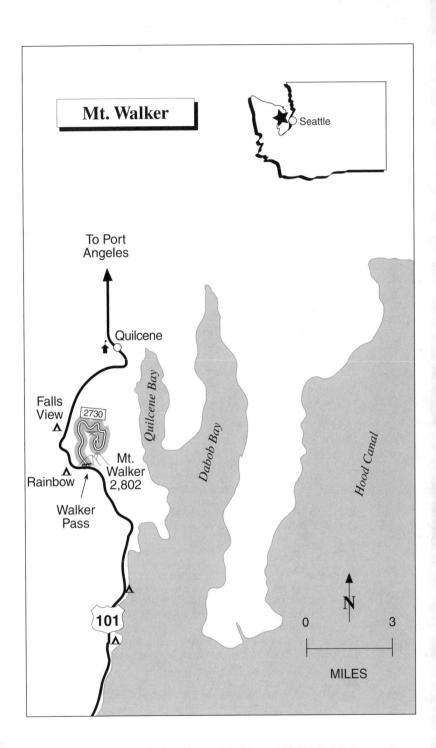

Mt. Walker

Seattle

To Port
Angeles

Quilcene

Quilcene Bay

Dabob Bay

Hood Canal

Falls
View

2730

Mt.
Walker
2,802

Rainbow

Walker
Pass

101

N

0   3

MILES

Queets River Road

LOCATION: The southwest corner of Olympic National Park. Jefferson County.

HIGHLIGHTS: Meander along one of the Olympic Peninsula's largest rivers, named for the Quiatso Indian tribe, on a little dead-end road through a temperate rain forest of ferns, flowers and mosses shaded by a canopy of towering conifers. The Queets River, fed by glacial meltwater from Mt. Olympus, is famous for steelhead fishing, and is popular for canoeing and kayaking as well. Watch for rare Roosevelt elk. Salmon may be seen spawning in the fall and winter as well. You can stop and search for one of the country's largest western hemlocks (227 feet tall and 291 inches in circumference), the Evergreen State's official state tree. At the end of the road, you can ford the river—on foot only, and only if conditions permit—and hike the popular Queets River Trail to see the park's largest Douglas fir (212 feet tall and 533.5 inches in circumference).

DIFFICULTY: Easy. But heavy rains and flooding can cause washouts and temporary closures.

TIME & DISTANCE: 2 hours; 27.6 miles round-trip.

MAPS: Olympic National Forest & National Park (D-F, 7-8). *Washington Road & Recreation Atlas*, p. 66 (D-E, 5-8).

INFORMATION: Olympic National Park. Queets Ranger Station (open seasonally), not far from the end of the road.

GETTING THERE: The road begins at the Jefferson-Grays Harbor county line, on the northeast side of U.S. 101 about 18 miles northwest of Lake Quinalt. Set your odometer to 0.

REST STOPS: Queets Campground, at the end of the road, has tent sites and a pit toilet, but no potable water.

THE DRIVE: In this part of the peninsula precipitation averages a soggy 120 inches a year in the lowlands, and 200 inches in the mountains. By comparison, the northeastern part of the peninsula, which lies in the mountains' moisture-sapped rain shadow, can receive as little as 15 inches a year. The effect of so much precipitation, as you will see, is an ecosystem teeming with life, one that is precious for having been spared the devastation of logging. In a coastal region where so much clearcutting has occurred, driving along an unspoiled rain forest valley, beside a pristine river like the Queets, is refreshing indeed. When you cross the bridge over Matheny Creek, note your odometer reading, and drive another 2.8 miles. Then look for one of the country's four tallest western hemlocks (the park has the three other "co-champions" as well, one of which, along the Hoh River Trail, is 241 feet tall), on the south side of the road. At the end of the road is the Queets River trailhead and the campground. To reach the park's largest Douglas fir, ford the river and follow the Queets River Trail 2.4 miles to Kloochman Rock Trail. Turn left at the junction, and hike another

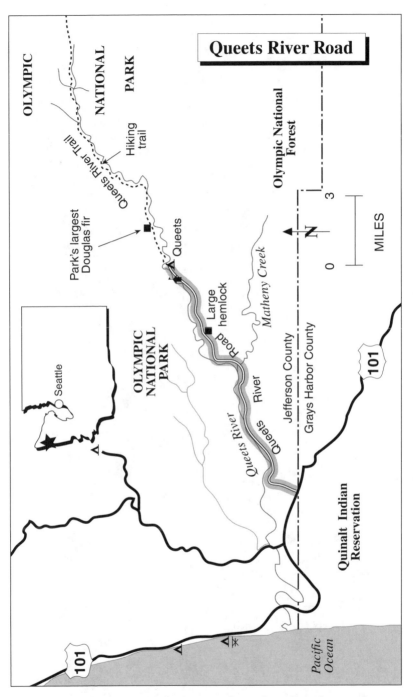

Queets River Road

0.2 mile. There is a sign where you leave the trail, and one at the tree.

37

Olympic Mountains (Tour 5)

Fording the Queets River (Tour 7)

Long Beach Peninsula

LOCATION: On the coast in Washington's far southwestern corner, just north of the mouth of the Columbia River. Pacific County.

HIGHLIGHTS: Long Beach claims the world's longest driveable beach, as well as fishing and clam digging (season varies; state permit required), and many other beach-oriented activities. An international kite festival is held here in August.

DIFFICULTY: Easy to difficult, on beach sand. Vehicles do get stuck sometimes, and a tow can cost at least $80. Air down your tires to 15 psi or so (air back up afterwards), and stick to the firmer wet sand. It's safest at low tide (pay attention to the tide). Speed limit is 25 mph. As signs state, the stretch of beach between the Long Beach and Seaview accesses is closed to motor vehicles from April 15 through the day after Labor Day. Do not drive near clam beds. The beach is considered a state highway, and all rules of the road apply.

TIME & DISTANCE: Take as long as you want to enjoy the 15-mile-long peninsula.

MAPS: Pick up a map at the Long Beach Peninsula Visitors Bureau, in Seaview. Local businesses have maps as well. Also see *Washington Road & Recreation Atlas*, p. 95 (B-F, 7).

INFORMATION: Long Beach Peninsula Visitors Bureau. Washington State Parks and Recreation Commission.

GETTING THERE: Take U.S. 101 to S.R. 103, north of the Columbia River. There are eight beach access points from S.R. 103: Seaview (38th Place), Long Beach (10th St. SW, Bolstad Ave. and N. 14th St.), Cranberry Road (between Long Beach and Loomis Lake State Park), Klipsan Beach (225th St.), Ocean Park (Bay Ave.) and Oysterville Road. Access roads in Seaview, Long Beach and Ocean Park can be jammed on summer weekends, so you might try the more remote accesses at Cranberry Road, Klipsan Beach and Oysterville Road.

REST STOPS: Campfires are OK at least 150 feet toward the shoreline from any beach grass. Overnight beach camping is not allowed, but there are many camping and lodging facilities within walking distance of the beach. The ocean is too cold and the surf too dangerous for swimming.

THE DRIVE: Few visitors drive the entire beach. Most use one of the access roads, then drive a short distance and park. Then they fish, ride horses or mountain bikes, stroll, and watch the setting sun. As beaches tend to do, this one, too, lets you define the experience for yourself. Do be considerate of others. Stay out of the soft, dry sand, which can swallow your wheels. And remember, the tide can come up fast.

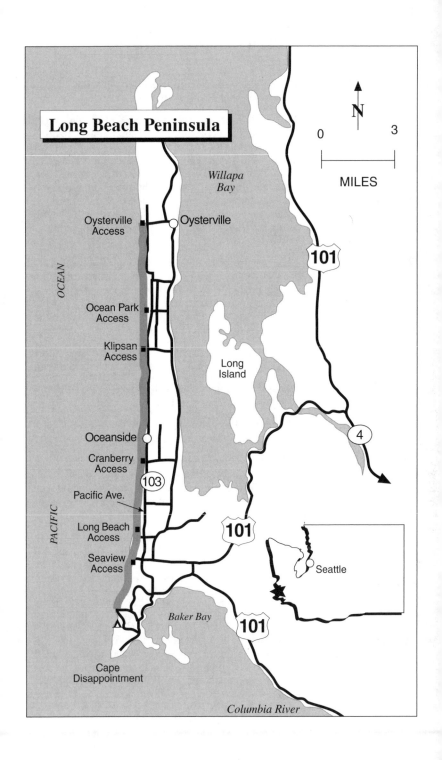

Long Beach Peninsula

OCEAN

PACIFIC

Willapa Bay

Oysterville Access
Oysterville

Ocean Park Access

Klipsan Access

Long Island

Oceanside

Cranberry Access

Pacific Ave.

Long Beach Access

Seaview Access

Baker Bay

Cape Disappointment

Columbia River

Seattle

N

0   3

MILES

101

4

103

101

101

Twin Lakes Road

LOCATION: Between S.R. 542 and the Canadian border. Mt. Baker-Snoqualmie National Forest. Whatcom County.

HIGHLIGHTS: This road packs more spectacular scenery per mile than any other in the book, but it is a source of contention between those who want vehicle access to the two pretty lakes for which it is named, and those who oppose it. It offers views of nearby 10,778-foot Mt. Baker, Goat Mountain, the glaciated Mt. Baker Wilderness and southern British Columbia. It ends at Twin Lakes, about 5,000 feet high, and the trail to 6,521-foot-high Winchester Mountain Lookout. Built in 1935 and staffed until 1966, it is maintained by the Mt. Baker Hiking Club. Bring a Northwest Forest Pass.

DIFFICULTY: Easy for the first 4.4 miles, on a maintained gravel road, then moderate on a small, rocky native-surface road with switchbacks. High clearance and 4WD are necessary for the last 2.4 miles or so. Watch for hikers. The road and the trail to the lookout are often blocked by snow until August. The hike to the lookout is strenuous, with an elevation gain of about 1,300 feet.

TIME & DISTANCE: 1.5 hours; 13.7 miles round-trip. Allow more than an hour (one way) for the 1.7-mile hike to the lookout.

MAPS: Mt. Baker-Snoqualmie National Forest (E, 1). *Washington Road & Recreation Atlas*, p. 43 (B, 8-9).

INFORMATION: Mt. Baker-Snoqualmie National Forest, Glacier Public Service Center, on S.R. 542 at Glacier.

GETTING THERE: From Bellingham, take S.R. 542 east through Glacier, toward Mt. Baker Ski Area and Artist Point. Twin Lakes Road (3065) begins on the north side of the highway at the state Department of Transportation facility. Set your odometer to 0 there.

REST STOPS: There is a pit toilet near the first of the Twin Lakes, and a couple of tables at the second. The grassy banks of the lakes are unprotected, so I don't recommend camping. The lookout is available for overnight stays (first-come, first-served).

THE DRIVE: Twin Lakes Road begins as a good, single-lane forest road that provides views of chiseled Goat Mountain and Mt. Baker, an active, snow-and-ice cloaked Cascade Range volcano. It is the second-most glaciated Cascade volcano, after Mt. Rainier, and the northernmost Cascade volcano in the United States. After 3.6 miles of climbing you will emerge from the forest and, if you stop and look back, you'll have a postcard-perfect view of it. At mile 4.4 is the popular Yellow Aster Butte trailhead, which leads into Mt. Baker Wilderness. (The entire road corridor is flanked by wilderness.) Beyond the trailhead the road is very rocky and narrow, but the views of angular Goat Mountain are terrific. Several switchbacks lie ahead. Soon you will reach the first of the Twin Lakes. The second lake is where the trail to the lookout begins. The road continues to an active gold-mining claim,

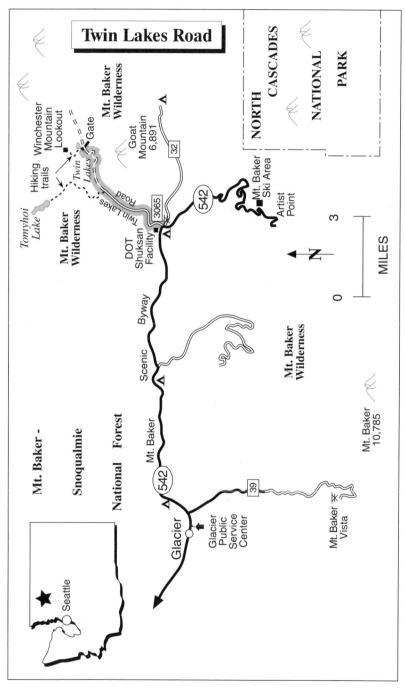

but access beyond the second lake is blocked by a locked gate. At the second lake a locked gate blocks the road, which leads to an active gold-mining claim. You can walk the road, however, for more majestic mountain views. If you hike to the lookout, go left where the trail forks.

Slate Peak

LOCATION: East of North Cascades National Park. Northwest of Winthrop. In a portion of Mt. Baker-Snoqualmie National Forest that is administered by Okanogan National Forest. Whatcom and Okanogan counties.

HIGHLIGHTS: Harts Pass Road, built to access a gold-mining district that boomed in the late 1800s and continued into the 1900s, will take you to a gorgeous alpine setting. It edges along a drop-off on a narrow shelf road in the North Cascades, then reaches Harts Pass. From there, the road to Slate Peak climbs above 7,000 feet to end at a tiny parking area that is the highest point in the state that you can drive to. To reach the occasionally staffed fire lookout atop 7,440-ft. Slate Peak, you'll have to hike the final steep quarter-mile segment of the road. But once there, visitors have expansive views of the North Cascades region. September is a beautiful time. You can combine this with Tour 11, Slate Creek Road.

DIFFICULTY: Easy, but rocky and narrow in places with blind curves. The road is typically open from early July through September. It's busy on weekends, so expect to encounter hikers and other vehicles, including stock trucks. Trailers are prohibited.

TIME & DISTANCE: 2 hours; 42 miles (round-trip) from Mazama. Allow time for the steep quarter-mile hike to the lookout.

MAPS: Okanogan National Forest (C-E, 2-3). *Washington Road & Recreation Atlas*, p. 45 (D-F, 7).

INFORMATION: Okanogan National Forest's Methow Valley Ranger District Visitor Information Center, on S.R. 20 west of central Winthrop. There's also a Forest Service guard station on Harts Pass.

GETTING THERE: Take S.R. 20 to Mazama, on the Methow River 13 miles northwest of Winthrop. Set your odometer to 0.

REST STOPS: There are two campgrounds near where the road begins the climb to Harts Pass, and two in the vicinity of the pass. The latter are primitive and waterless, but for seasonal springs.

THE DRIVE: From Mazama, Lost River Road (1183) courses up the glacier-dozed valley of the Methow River. The pavement ends 6.7 miles from Mazama. A couple of miles beyond that, at the turnoff to River Bend Campground, turn right, onto Harts Pass Road (5400). Harts Pass Road climbs, narrows to a heart-stopping shelf, and runs along a sheer cliff. Here, you can gaze across Methow Valley at the peaks of the national park. Soon you will be back on a typical maintained forest road. You'll know you're at Harts Pass (about 6,200 feet) when you see a ranger station. Road 600 to Slate Peak is to the right here (ahead is Slate Creek Road). Road 600 climbs to the parking area below the lookout. (The parking area may be full on busy days.) The lookout was built in 1956, after the Air Force blasted 40 feet from the peak for a radar station that wasn't built.

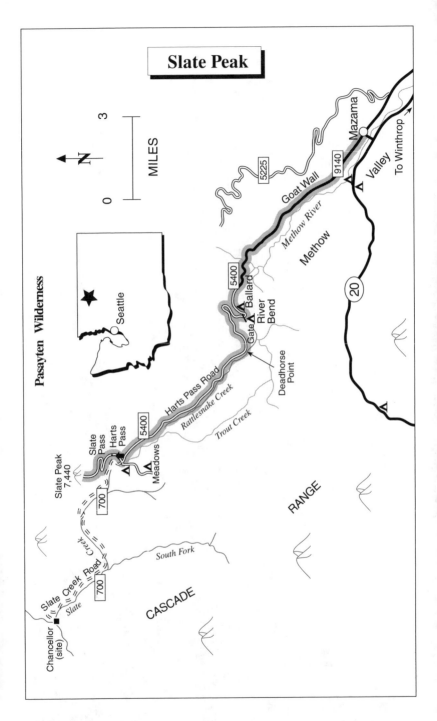

Slate Peak

MILES

0 3

N

Pasayten Wilderness

Seattle

Slate Peak 7,440

Slate Pass

Harts Pass

5400

700

Slate Creek Road

700

Chancellor (site)

South Fork

Slate Creek

CASCADE

RANGE

Harts Pass Road

Rattlesnake Creek

Trout Creek

Meadows

Gate

Ballard

River Bend

5400

Deadhorse Point

Methow River

Methow

Goat Wall

5225

9140

Mazama

To Winthrop

Valley

20

ALSO TRY: Road 5225, north of Mazama and east of Lost River Road, goes to the top of a 2,500-foot cliff, Goat Wall, for a view of Methow Valley. Sweetgrass Butte, northwest of Winthrop, also provides a panorama of the region.

Twin Lakes (Tour 9)

Harts Pass Road (Tours 10 & 11)

Slate Creek Road

LOCATION: East of North Cascades National Park. Northwest of Winthrop. Okanogan National Forest. Whatcom County.

HIGHLIGHTS: After making the exhilarating trek up to Harts Pass (Tour 10), you will plunge into the narrow, steep-walled canyon of Slate Creek, following a road that miners, hikers and backcountry explorers have traveled since gold was discovered in the area in 1880. Relics from the late 19th and early 20th century, such as old mine sites, town sites and dilapidated structures, still dot the mountains. You will pass a number of active claims, although much of the activity today is recreational rather than entrepreneurial. The drive ends in 5.4 miles, at an old log-supported bridge over Slate Creek that the Forest Service says is no longer safe for vehicles larger than ATVs, motorcycles and mountain bikes. You can hike or ride from there for another 5 miles, to road's end at the site of Chancellor, one of the area's several short-lived boom towns. You can combine this trip with the drive to Slate Peak (also Tour 10).

DIFFICULTY: Easy but a bit rough, on a narrow single-lane native-surface road requiring high ground clearance. It's typically open from early July through September.

TIME & DISTANCE: 1 hour; 10.8 miles round-trip from Harts Pass.

MAPS: Okanogan National Forest (C-D, 2-3). *Washington Road & Recreation Atlas*, pp. 44-45 (D, 6-7).

INFORMATION: Okanogan National Forest's Methow Valley Ranger District Visitor Information Center, on S.R. 20 west of central Winthrop. There's a Forest Service guard station on Harts Pass.

GETTING THERE: Take S.R. 20 to Mazama, on the Methow River 13 miles northwest of Winthrop. From Mazama, follow the directions to Harts Pass provided in Tour 10. At the pass, where the road to Slate Peak (600) bends to the right past the Forest Service guard station, Slate Creek Road (700) continues directly ahead. Set your odometer to 0 there.

REST STOPS: Harts Pass and Meadows campgrounds. There are primitive campsites along Slate Creek, but don't use the mining claims that are posted along the creek.

THE DRIVE: The narrow, rocky old road descends rapidly and fairly steeply into the heavily forested canyon, whose close, steep walls contrast with the expansive views you can take in from nearby Slate Peak. About 3.6 miles from Harts Pass you'll cross a small bridge over Slate Creek, and then pass several mining claims, which some folks use as weekend getaways as much as anything. After driving alongside Slate Creek for 5.4 miles, you will reach the old bridge described under "Highlights." You can park here, and continue to the site of Chancellor afoot or by bike to continue your North Cascades outing.

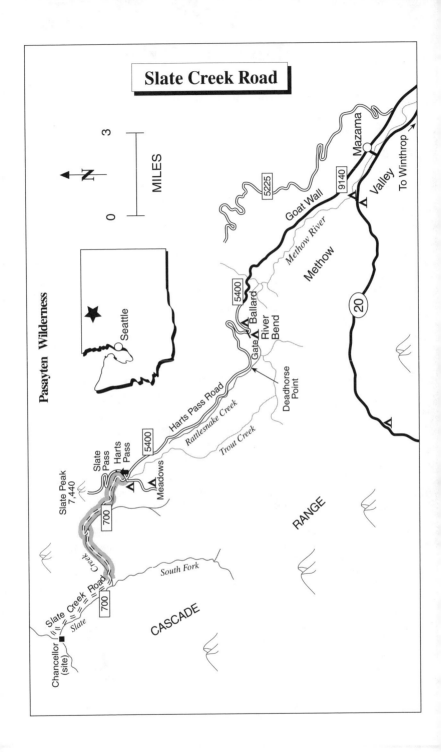

Slate Creek Road

Pasayten Wilderness

Lone Frank Pass

LOCATION: Northwest of Conconully, in the foothills east of the Cascade Range. Okanogan National Forest and Loomis State Forest. Okanogan County.

HIGHLIGHTS: A strong sense of remoteness and a range of impressive scenery make this trip especially appealing. You will pass through pastoral meadows, forests of pine, aspen and fir, and vast, eerie expanses of burned forest. The area is noted for its wildflower displays in June and July. From elevations that approach 7,000 feet, you'll also have terrific views that stretch from the North Cascades eastward to the Columbia Basin.

DIFFICULTY: Easy, on gravel and native-surface roads. There are rocky segments that require high ground clearance.

TIME & DISTANCE: 1.5 hours; 25.5 miles.

MAPS: Okanogan National Forest (K-L, 2-3). *Washington Road & Recreation Atlas*, p. 46 (C-F, 3-4).

INFORMATION: Okanogan National Forest's Tonasket Ranger District.

GETTING THERE: From Conconully, take North Fork Salmon Creek Road/Forest Highway 38 north to Salmon Meadows Campground (8.5 miles). Set your odometer to 0 there.

REST STOPS: Salmon Meadows (a particularly pleasant place) and Long Swamp campgrounds. There are other campgrounds in the area as well, including Conconully State Park.

THE DRIVE: From pretty Salmon Meadows, road 3820, a typical native-surface forest road, begins a long, steady climb amid rolling hills wooded with pines and stands of aspen that promise early-autumn color. Glance to the east, and you'll see the vast, pale and considerably drier steppes that lie in the rain shadow of the Cascade Range, which etches the skyline to the west. About 5.3 miles from Salmon Meadows, where the road crosses a corner of Loomis State Forest, you'll go over Lone Frank Pass, which my altimeter registered at about 6,900 feet. Soon you will come to gravel road 39. Follow it north, toward Long Swamp. In the coming miles the road will take you past Twentymile Meadows, and then through Thirtymile Meadows. Both are serene, grassy expanses drained by similarly named creeks that flow west into the Chewuch River. The beauty of these meadows contrasts dramatically with the haunting expanses of charred forest left by the Thunder Fire in 1994. The road passes through this monochromatic firescape, and reaches Long Swamp Campground in about 8 miles. There, the paved leg of road 39 descends east along Toats Coulee to beautiful Sinlahekin Valley and the hamlet of Loomis.

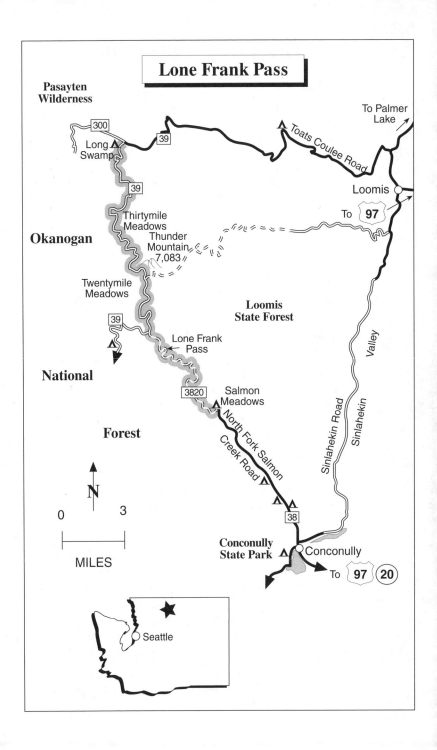

Lone Frank Pass

Pasayten
Wilderness

300

39

Long
Swamp

To Palmer
Lake

Toats Coulee Road

Loomis

To 97

39

Okanogan

Thirtymile
Meadows
Thunder
Mountain
7,083

Twentymile
Meadows

Loomis
State Forest

39

Lone Frank
Pass

National

3820

Salmon
Meadows

Forest

North Fork Salmon
Creek Road

Sinlahekin Road

Sinlahekin

Valley

N

0   3

MILES

38

Conconully
State Park

Conconully

To 97 20

Seattle

Chopaka Lake Road

LOCATION: The eastern slope of the Cascades in north-central Washington, just south of the Canadian border. Loomis State Forest, northwest of Loomis. Okanogan County.

HIGHLIGHTS: Fly fishers can cast for rainbow trout in Chopaka Lake, an irrigation reservoir named for an Indian word meaning "high mountain." The descent from the lake to Sinlahekin Valley provides fine views of this geologically tumultuous region. You may even see bighorn sheep on the slopes you'll cross on the way down.

DIFFICULTY: Easy, on a maintained gravel road.

TIME & DISTANCE: 1 hour; 19 miles. The spur to Cold Springs viewpoint adds about 45 minutes and 5.8 miles (round-trip).

MAPS: Okanogan National Forest (L-M, 1-2). *Washington Road & Recreation Atlas*, p. 46 (B-C, 5-6).

INFORMATION: Bureau of Land Management's Wenatchee Field Office. Okanogan County.

GETTING THERE: From Loomis, west of U.S. 97 at the northern end of Sinlahekin Valley, take Loomis-Oroville Road north for 2 miles. Turn left (west) onto Toats Coulee Road (39). In 1.4 miles you'll see, on the right, a turnoff to Chopaka Lake (about 8.4 miles from here). This is where you'll come out. Pass the turnoff and drive 7 more miles. Turn right (north) at the sign for Cold Springs and Fourteen Mile Trailhead. Set your odometer to 0.

REST STOPS: Chopaka Lake, Cold Springs and North Fork Ninemile campgrounds. There is a picnic area and toilet at the Cold Springs viewpoint.

THE DRIVE: The road climbs amid hills of sagebrush and grass, and brings you to a junction. Go right, to Chopaka Lake Road. About 3.7 miles farther is the left (northwest) turn to Cold Springs Campground and viewpoint. Here, Chopaka Lake Road angles to the southeast and descends through forest, with views of mountains and hills to the east. On the left about 4.5 miles from the Cold Springs turnoff is road 2400. It goes 2 miles to Chopaka Lake, which occupies something of a high bowl surrounded by pretty, wooded hills and peaks. The campground there isn't the best, but it is free, and it's popular among anglers (fly fishing only; no motors). Your route descends from this junction through hills of sagebrush, pine and aspen, becoming a wide mountainside shelf as it takes you back to Toats Coulee Road.

Chopaka Lake Road

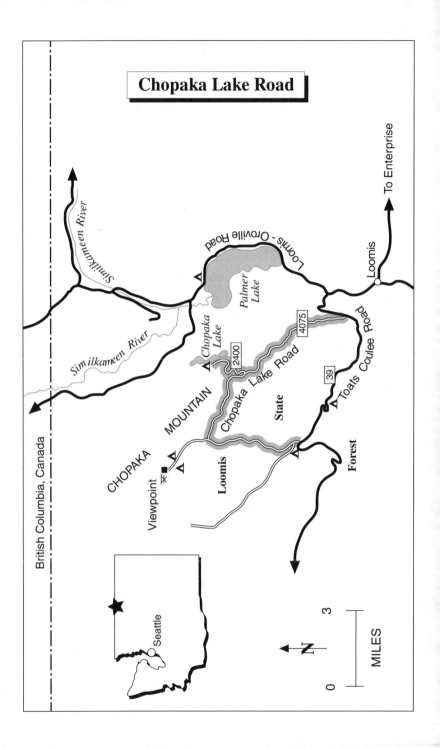

Ellemeham Mountain Road

LOCATION: North-central Washington just south of the Canadian border. Okanogan County, west of Oroville.

HIGHLIGHTS: West of the confluence of the Similkameen and Okanogan rivers rise beautiful but austere hills, bluffs, canyons and cliffs. The banks and gravel bars of the Similkameen, just to the north of this old mining and ranching road, were the focus of an 1860s gold rush. Today, the hills that flank the river, including those along this trip, remain pocked with old gold and silver mines, some of which were worked into the 20th century.

DIFFICULTY: Easy, on a maintained gravel road.

TIME & DISTANCE: 1 hour; 19 miles.

MAPS: Okanogan National Forest (N, 1). *Washington Road & Recreation Atlas*, p. 47 (A-B, 7-8).

INFORMATION: Okanogan County.

GETTING THERE: As the maps noted above show, there are a number of ways to take this drive. To go the way I describe: In Oroville, take 12th Avenue (old Highway 7) south from Main Street (U.S. 97) for about 2.8 miles, then turn right (west) at the sign for Golden Road. Take Golden Road a short way west and north. Turn left (west) onto Blue Lake Road, toward Wannacut Lake. Set the odometer to 0.

REST STOPS: If you're an angler, Wannacut and Blue lakes offer trout fishing. Nearby Oroville has all services.

THE DRIVE: Blue Lake Road is paved for 0.6 mile, then it becomes a manicured gravel road. Follow it west into the rumpled hills, past Blue Lake and through a rock-walled canyon. Shortly beyond the north end of Wannacut Lake, Wannacut Lake Road comes in from the south (left) to meet Blue Lake Road. Continue ahead, on what is now Wannacut Lake Road, and the route will bend north and climb into Hicks Canyon. At a bend in the road in 2.4 miles, you will see a little road coming in from the east (right). It's Ellis Barnes Road, shown on some maps as a rudimentary leg of Ellemeham Mountain Road. The much better road ahead is Ellemeham Mountain Road as well; I recommend going that way, through hills of sagebrush and aspen and up a narrow draw. All around at this point are high, terraced mountainsides and range-lands, all of which create a serene landscape that takes on a golden hue in the light of late afternoon. Another narrow canyon follows as the road heads east, along an aspen-lined creek. Eventually you will be gazing down at Blue and Mud lakes from a high vantage point. From there, the road winds down into the valley of the Okanogan River, where glacier-carved rock terraces loom over a quilt of verdant orchards. All too soon you will be back on paved Golden Road, with old Highway 7 just up ahead.

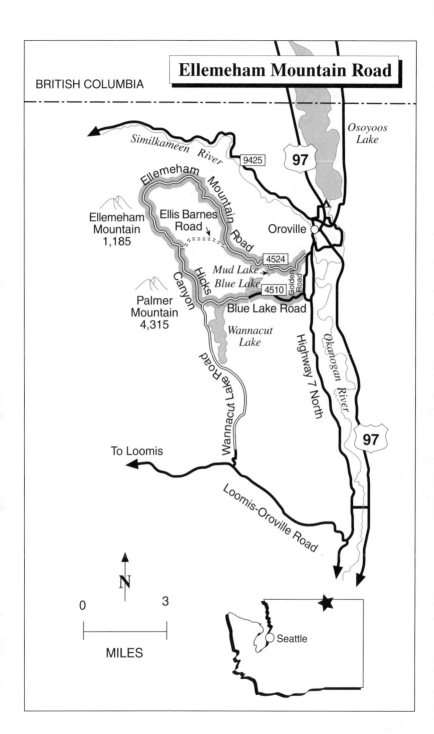

Ellemeham Mountain Road

BRITISH COLUMBIA

Osoyoos Lake

Similkameen River

9425

97

Ellemeham Mountain Road

Ellemeham Mountain 1,185

Ellis Barnes Road

Oroville

4524

Mud Lake
Blue Lake

4510

Golden Road

Palmer Mountain 4,315

Hicks Canyon

Blue Lake Road

Wannacut Lake

Highway 7 North

Okanogan River

Wannacut Lake Road

97

To Loomis

Loomis-Oroville Road

N

0   3

MILES

Seattle

Washburn Lake Road

LOCATION: Northeast of Loomis, on the southern slope of Palmer Mountain in north-central Washington, near the Canadian border. Okanogan County.

HIGHLIGHTS: Although this is a short drive, it will take you into beautiful, rolling sagebrush country. The views of the mountains and deep valleys of Okanogan County are outstanding.

DIFFICULTY: Easy, on a gravel-and-dirt road.

TIME & DISTANCE: 1 hour; 9.4 miles round-trip.

MAPS: *Washington Road & Recreation Atlas*, p. 47 (C, 7). Okanogan National Forest (N, 2).

INFORMATION: Bureau of Land Management's Wenatchee Field Office.

GETTING THERE: Take Loomis-Oroville Road to the west end of Spectacle Lake, 2.4 miles east of the hamlet of Loomis. Turn north at the apple orchard.

REST STOPS: Primitive camping is available at Washburn Lake, a small lake that is stocked with eastern brook trout.

THE DRIVE: At the outset, if you look carefully along the base of the mountain, you'll see the remains of an old wooden irrigation flume once used to water the area's orchards. The road begins a steady and fairly steep climb immediately upon leaving Loomis-Oroville Road, providing views of rolling, rugged and almost desert-like hills. At mile 2.9 from Loomis-Oroville Road, Washburn Lake Road passes through a stand of large aspens, which blaze with golden hues in late summer or early autumn. By about mile 4 you'll see small two-tracks branching off the main road. As the signposts indicate, they've been closed to motor vehicles since the BLM acquired thousands of acres around Washburn Lake in 1995. Obey the closures. At mile 4.7 the road ends in a parking and camping area just short of the small lake.

WASHBURN LAKE ROAD

Washburn Lake Road

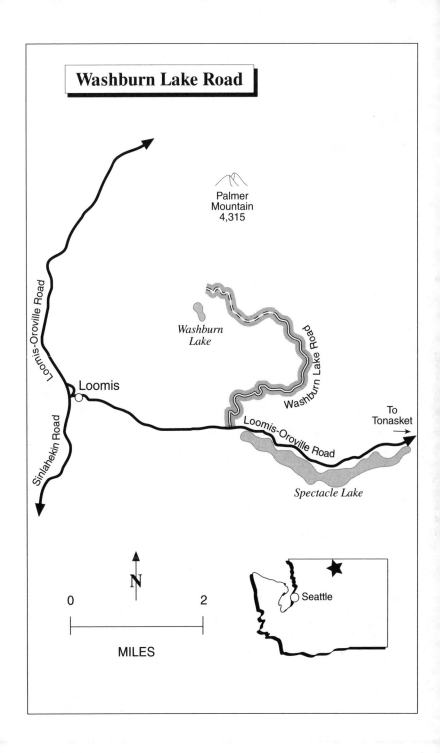

Palmer Mountain 4,315

Loomis-Oroville Road

Washburn Lake

Washburn Lake Road

Loomis

Sinlahekin Road

Loomis-Oroville Road

To Tonasket →

Spectacle Lake

N

0 2

MILES

Seattle

Sinlahekin Road

LOCATION: South of Loomis on the eastern slope of the Cascade Range, in north-central Washington just south of the Canadian border. Okanogan County.

HIGHLIGHTS: Sinlahekin Valley is another of Washington's beautiful glacial troughs, with high and steep walls that tower above Sinlahekin Creek and the Sinlahekin Wildlife Area. Access to the creek (by foot) is difficult, but it is known for brook and rainbow trout. Blue Lake, about midway, is good for rainbow and brown trout, while Fish Lake, at the south end, is good for rainbow.

DIFFICULTY: Easy, on a maintained gravel road. Fish Lake/-Pine Creek Road is paved. Watch for logging trucks.

TIME & DISTANCE: 1 hour or less; 26 miles.

MAPS: Okanogan National Forest (M-N, 2-4). *Washington Road & Recreation Atlas*, p. 46 (C-F, 6).

INFORMATION: Okanogan County. Washington Department of Fish & Wildlife.

GETTING THERE: Take this drive north or south. Either way is gorgeous. **To go south**: Get to Loomis, southwest of Oroville and south of Palmer Lake. Go west through town, then turn south on Sinlahekin Road. **To go north:** Take S.R. 20/U.S. 97 about 5.6 miles north from Riverside. Turn west on Pine Creek Road. Head west to Fish Lake and Sinlahekin Road.

REST STOPS: There is primitive camping at Blue Lake, Connors Lake, Forde Lake and Fish Lake. At the south end of the drive you won't be far from Conconully State Park, which also has camping and fishing.

THE DRIVE: Thousands of years ago, massive glaciers bulldozed their way through today's Washington, sculpting many of the landscapes we most appreciate today, from Puget Sound to the Cascade Range and the Selkirks. Among them, too, is the 17-mile-long, north-south Sinlahekin Valley, where a glacier's path is obvious from walls that rise steeply more than 3,000 feet above the rolling valley floor. On the valley floor is Sinlahekin Creek, which links several small and rather algae-choked lakes as it meanders through stands of birch, willow and aspen. Watch for beaver ponds and dams as well. Higher up is more open country, with ponderosa pine and bunchgrass, bitterbrush and chokecherry. The valley is the heart of the 13,814-acre Sinlahekin Wildlife Area. The state's oldest wildlife area, it provides habitat for a wide range of wildlife, including mule deer, raptors, waterfowl and coyotes.

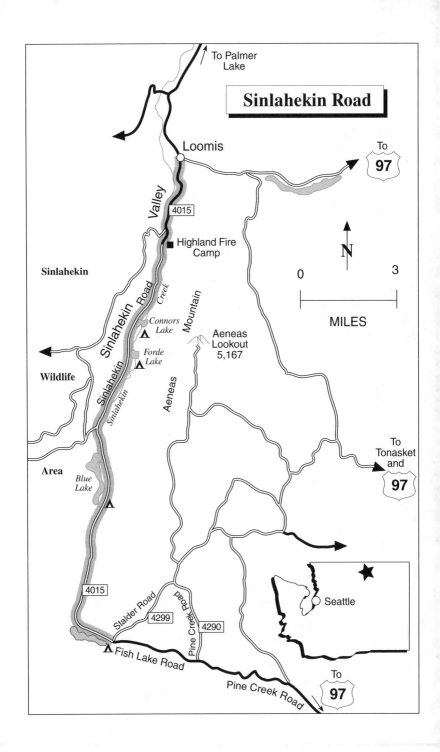

To Palmer
Lake

Sinlahekin Road

Loomis

To
97

4015

Highland Fire
Camp

N

0   3

Sinlahekin

MILES

Connors
Lake

Aeneas
Lookout
5,167

Forde
Lake

Wildlife

To
Tonasket
and
97

Area

Blue
Lake

Fish Lake Road

4015

Stalder Road

4299

Pine Creek Road

4290

Seattle

Pine Creek Road

To
97

Baldy Pass

LOCATION: Northeast of Winthrop, northwest of Conconully. Okanogan National Forest. Okanogan County.

HIGHLIGHTS: You will travel along the Chewuch River, where salmon can be seen spawning in August, then climb into rugged mountains for spectacular vistas from Baldy Pass (6,515 feet) and the lookout on First Butte (5,491 feet).

DIFFICULTY: Easy, on a mix of single-lane dirt-and-gravel and asphalt roads. Watch for logging trucks. The road is usually open May-October.

TIME & DISTANCE: 2.5 hours; about 51 miles.

MAPS: Okanogan National Forest (J-L, 3-4). *Washington Road & Recreation Atlas*, p. 46 (F-G, 1-5).

INFORMATION: Okanogan National Forest's Methow Valley Ranger District. Methow Valley Visitor Information Center, on S.R. 20 just west of downtown Winthrop.

GETTING THERE: From central Winthrop (the way I take you): Set our odometer to 0, then take Riverside Street north. Riverside Street will become Bluff Street. Follow the signs toward Pearrygin Lake State Park. The road will become East Chewuch Road (9137), which you will follow. **From Conconully:** At the junction of West Fork Road (2017) and Conconully Road (at Conconully State Park), go right (west). Take West Fork Road for 3.1 miles, then turn right (northwest) on road 37.

REST STOPS: First Butte Lookout.

THE DRIVE: From Winthrop, the paved road meanders north along the Chewuch River for about 6.6 miles. Turn right (northeast) onto road 37, a paved single-lane road along aptly named Boulder Creek. In 6 miles the pavement ends, and you'll soon see road 800 branching to the left (north). To visit First Butte Lookout, built in 1938, take road 800 for 2.4 miles, then go left (southwest), and drive 2.2 miles to the lookout. There, you can gaze across the rugged North Cascades region, including the national park and Pasayten Wilderness. Return to road 37, and continue for almost 6 miles to the junction with road 39. Go right (southeast) on road 37, now single-lane dirt, and climb 5.6 miles to Baldy Pass. This leg provides terrific views of the rocky 7,844-foot peak of Old Baldy, and west to the North Cascades. Descending from the pass, the road becomes a narrow shelf for a bit. Stop along the way, and look out across the eastern Cascades' foothills and the long brown valleys of the Columbia Basin. Asphalt resumes 9.3 miles below the pass, and 5 miles farther is a junction. Go left (northeast) here, onto West Fork Road. In 3.1 miles you'll be in Conconully.

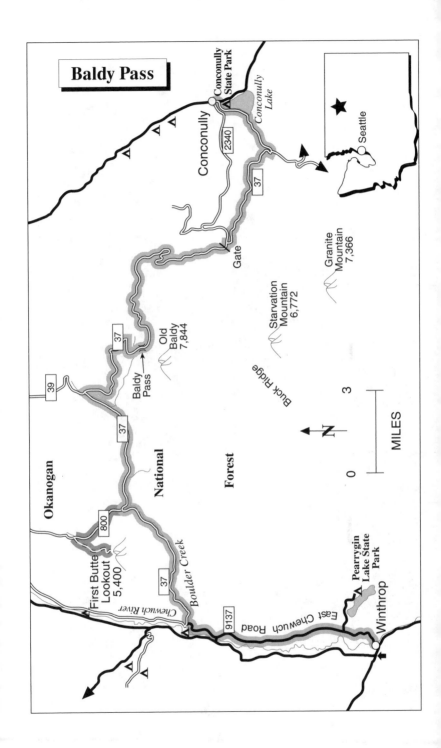

Bighorn sheep (Tour 13)

Old Molson (Tour 18)

Molson Loop

LOCATION: North-central Washington's Okanogan Highlands, east of Oroville and just south of the Canadian border. Okanogan County.

HIGHLIGHTS: This bucolic cruise goes up to the Canadian border, passing a number of historic features: Old Molson, where locals preserve a cluster of historic buildings; the Molson School (1914-1962); the site of bygone Sidley, British Columbia; and old railroad grades and road cuts that recall the days when smoke, steam and whistles filled the highland air and Molson had Washington's highest railroad depot (3,708 feet). You will gaze across a broad upland that once lay beneath a continental ice sheet. Geologists theorize that this was once the Okanogan microcontinent, a fragment of the Pangaea supercontinent that broke apart 200 million years ago. North America's former western shore lies to the east, where the Columbia River now flows. About 100 million years ago, the eastward-moving Okanogan microcontinent collided with the westward-moving North American continent, beginning the assembling of Washington and British Columbia. Then some 50 million years ago, the eastward-moving North Cascades microcontinent collided with the western edge of the Okanogan microcontinent, at today's Okanogan Valley.

DIFFICULTY: Easy. Half of it is paved. The rest is gravel.

TIME & DISTANCE: 1 hour; 15.8 miles.

MAPS: AAA's *Oregon & Washington* (E, 23). *Washington Road & Recreation Atlas*, p. 47 (A-B, 9-10).

INFORMATION: Okanogan County Historical Society.

GETTING THERE: From Main Street/U.S. 97 in central Oroville, turn east onto Central Avenue and follow the signs for the Molson Museum. When you reach Oroville-Toroda Creek Road, follow it east for almost 10 miles, then turn north (left) onto Molson Road. You'll see a sign for the museum. Set your odometer to 0.

REST STOPS: The friendly folks who staff the Molson School Museum sell homemade refreshments.

THE DRIVE: After driving north for 5 miles through the hills of Mud Lake Valley, you will reach Old Molson, a collection of historic structures—the bank, assay office, cabins and such. The site is a reminder of a time when the international border just up the road didn't mean much to the farm families of the Okanogan Highlands. Old Molson was founded in 1900 as a mining camp. When a farmer claimed it was on his land, residents moved it a half mile up the road, to today's Molson. The camp died out in 1901. Then homesteaders arrived. The railroad arrived in 1905, turning Molson into a commercial hub that extended into Canada. After stopping at the school, drive past Molson Lake, where the asphalt ends, and head west on Nine Mile Road. Soon you'll see a sign denoting the site of Sidley, B.C., which existed just north

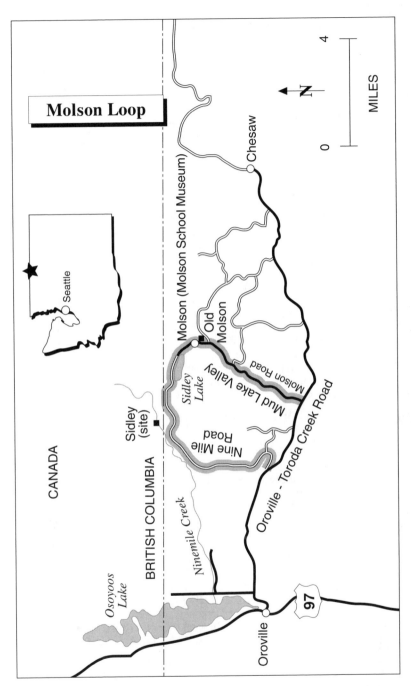

Molson Loop

of the international border (a few yards north of the road) from 1895 to 1912. The jagged Cascades loom to the west. As you approach Oroville-Toroda Creek Road again, you will pass through narrow road cuts once used by steam-powered trains, and see sections of the old railroad grade, which was abandoned in 1935. Finally, the road passes the site of Circle City, where Oroville-bound trains paused to cool their brakes.

Bamber Creek-Trout Creek

LOCATION: West of Curlew, in northeastern Washington just south of the Canadian border. Colville National Forest. Ferry County.

HIGHLIGHTS: This gentle forest-lover's journey climbs about 2,000 feet, providing views of the beautiful Kettle River valley.

DIFFICULTY: Easy. The roadbed is primarily gravel, with a stretch of two-track native dirt.

TIME & DISTANCE: 1 hour; 22.6 miles.

MAPS: Colville National Forest, West Half (B-C, 1-3). *Washington Road & Recreation Atlas*, p. 48 (B-C, 4).

INFORMATION: Colville National Forest's Republic Ranger District.

GETTING THERE: From the north (the way I describe): Make your way toward the junction of Toroda Creek Road (502) and West Kettle River Road (525), west of S.R. 21 and a few miles south of the Canadian border. About a mile south of the junction, turn west off West Kettle River Road onto Bamber Creek Road (523), set your odometer to 0, and drive past the Curlew Civilian Conservation/Job Corps Center. **From the south:** Head to Curlew Lake, and West Curlew Lake Road (203). Turn west onto paved Trout Creek Road (201).

REST STOPS: You shouldn't need one on this short drive. There are many primitive campsites along the way, and Curlew Lake State Park has camping.

THE DRIVE: Bamber Creek Road is paved to the conservation center, then becomes gravel as it begins the long climb into the forested mountains. About 2.8 miles from West Kettle River Road you'll have a terrific vista across the river valley far below. In another mile the road enters the national forest, where its number changes to 800. A mile more, and it diminishes to a dirt two-track. Soon you will edge along a narrow shelf, then come to roads 2148 and 2149. You can take either road southward, but I suggest following 2148 southwest (to the right), along Tonata Creek, which seems more scenic to me. The road will become gravel again, and make a long bend around Kelly Mountain. Then it angles southeast, leaves the national forest and connects with 2149. Continue south along Trout Creek, on what becomes road 517, which leads to Trout Creek Road (201) and West Curlew Lake Road.

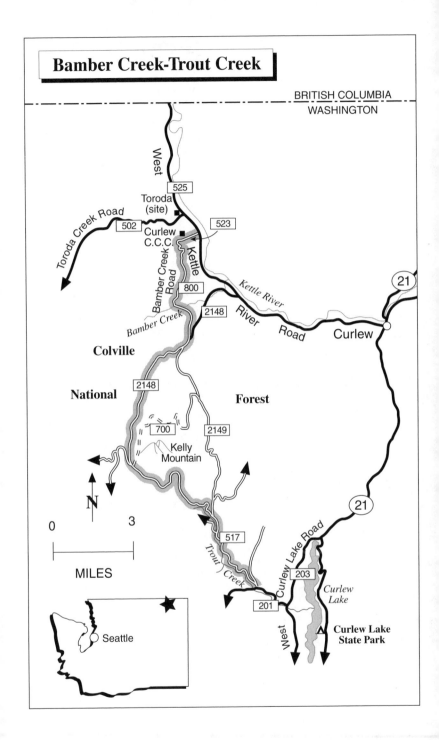

Bamber Creek-Trout Creek

Refrigerator Canyon Loop

LOCATION: In the Kettle River Range southeast of Republic and south of S.R. 20. Colville National Forest. Ferry County.

HIGHLIGHTS: This trip samples part of a region that some conservationists want declared either a national monument or something close to a wilderness area to protect old-growth forest and roadless tracts. You will experience the closeness of the forests, particularly in beautiful Refrigerator Canyon (where temperatures tend to be at least 10 degrees cooler than the surrounding area), as well as broad vistas. Nine Mile Falls can be viewed from the road, or you can take the short hike to a viewing platform. The massive washout of Refrigerator Canyon Road (233), which occurred during a spring flood in 1998, is an impressive sight.

DIFFICULTY: Easy, on narrow, high-clearance dirt-and-gravel roads. Two-track McMann Creek Road (500) is more rudimentary and rockier than the others, but still easy. The washed-out northern end of Refrigerator Canyon Road, south of Hall Creek Road (99), is impassable. Access to the canyon is from the south, via Quartz Ridge Road (2053). The hike to Nine Mile Falls is moderately strenuous.

TIME & DISTANCE: 1.5 hours; 27.8 miles. If you take McMann Creek Road (500) instead of Quartz Ridge Road (2053), deduct 4.4 miles. Add 20 minutes (round-trip) for the hike to Nine Mile Falls.

MAPS: Colville National Forest, West Half (C-D, 4). *Washington Road & Recreation Atlas*, p. 48 (F-G, 4-5).

INFORMATION: Colville National Forest's Republic Ranger District.

GETTING THERE: From Republic, take S.R. 20 southeast for 7 miles, to Hall Creek Road (99). Turn right (south). Set your odometer to 0. This access, described below, has fine vistas to the west and south. A different yet appealing access is 4.2-mile McMann Creek Road (500), a pretty little road. To reach it, from the junction of S.R. 20 and S.R. 21, take S.R. 21 south for about 5.7 miles. Turn left (east). Take the rocky little road between two private driveways.

REST STOPS: Nine Mile Falls.

THE DRIVE: From S.R. 20, take Hall Creek Road 0.3 mile, then turn right (west) onto Quartz Ridge Road (2053). Climbing gradually, the road winds through forest on the flanks of Quartz Mountain, providing views across seemingly endless low, rumpled mountains. In 8.3 miles is the junction with McMann Creek Road, on the right. Continuing south, east and then northeast, you will reach Refrigerator Canyon Road (233) in 5 miles. Road 2053 continues to the right (south and east). For now, drive 2 miles up Refrigerator Canyon, below its high, rocky walls. The road ends at a roadblock, where you can gaze down at the massive washout. Backtrack to 2053, and take it 1.6 miles to the junction with

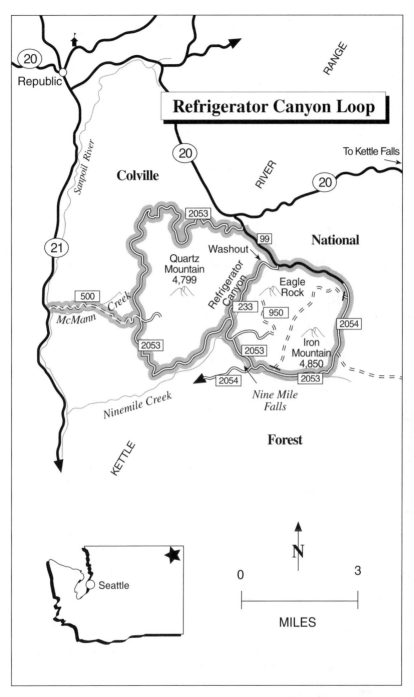

Refrigerator Canyon Loop

Thirteenmile Road (2054). Here you can see Nine Mile Falls below the road. There's an information kiosk at the trailhead. (The hike to the falls follows a gentle downhill grade.) From here, continue east and north, on roads 2053 and 2054. In 6.6 miles you'll pass Quartz Ridge Road and, in another 0.3 mile, you'll be back at S.R. 20.

Flat Creek-Pierre Creek

LOCATION: Just south of the Canadian border in Washington's northeastern corner, between the Columbia River and U.S. 395. Colville National Forest. Stevens County.

HIGHLIGHTS: You'll enjoy terrific views of the Columbia River Gorge and the high, golden-brown benchlands, rolling rangelands and bucolic valleys that flank it.

DIFFICULTY: Easy, on road surfaces that range from asphalt and graded gravel to rocky native surfaces.

TIME & DISTANCE: 1 hour; 24 miles.

MAPS: Colville National Forest, West Half (G-J, 1-2). *Washington Road & Recreation Atlas*, pp. 49 (B, 9-12) & 50 (B-C, 1-3).

INFORMATION: Colville National Forest's Three Rivers Ranger District.

GETTING THERE: Find your way to the Columbia River town of Northport, on S.R. 25 a few miles south of the Canadian border. Cross the river bridge, set your odometer to 0, and drive southwest along the river on mostly paved Northport-Flat Creek Road (4005).

REST STOPS: Pierre Lake Campground, near the western terminus of the trip.

THE DRIVE: Northport-Flat Creek Road crosses picturesque benchlands high above the great Columbia River, providing outstanding views of the gorge's cliffs and bluffs as well as the hills and steep mountains beyond. At a cattleguard 10.7 miles from S.R. 25, turn right (north) on gravel Lael (a.k.a. Flat Creek) Road (county road 4181/forest road 1520), which follows Flat Creek. From here, the road passes through a ranch, then takes you into golden-hued, rocky and rumpled hills. Soon you will pass some old ranch buildings. Beyond them the road diminishes to a single lane of dirt and gravel, and climbs into the hills via a long, wooded valley. The forest will close in, creating a tunnel effect, once you cross the marked national forest boundary. About 4.5 miles from the forest boundary is a small junction; go left (southwest), continuing on road 4181/1520. The Forest Service's road number will soon change to 020. In another 5.1 miles, as the road follows Pierre Creek, is another junction. Road 15 is on the right, and road 080 on the left. Continue straight ahead, staying on road 4181/020, which now becomes a very good, graded-gravel road. In another 1.5 miles you will emerge into another beautiful valley, at paved Pierre Lake Road (4013). The lake, and its campground, are to the left (south). U.S. 395 is about 4 miles farther west, via paved Sand Creek Road (4013).

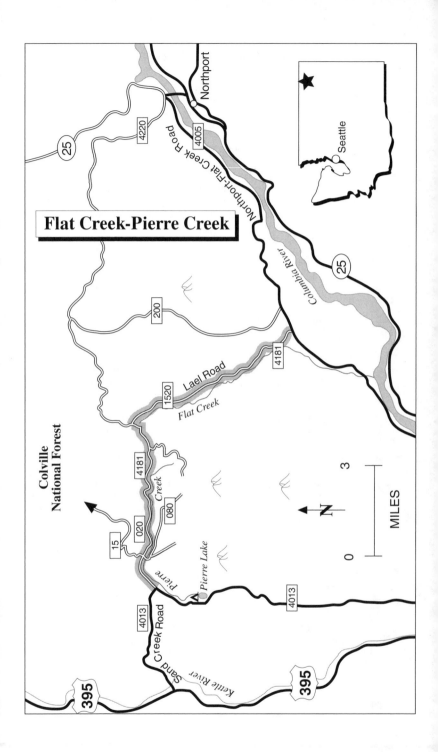

Flat Creek-Pierre Creek

Bangs Mountain

LOCATION: Northwestern Washington, south of S.R. 20 between Sherman Pass and the Columbia River (Franklin Roosevelt Lake). Colville National Forest. Ferry County.

HIGHLIGHTS: This short trip along Canyon Creek Road will take you through Donaldson Draw, a rocky reminder of the time when ice sheets thousands of feet thick blanketed much of North America. The road ends atop Bangs Mountain, at a vista point more than 3,000 feet high, from which you can peer out across the vast, semiarid volcanic steppe of the Columbia Basin.

DIFFICULTY: Easy, on a single-lane dirt road.

TIME & DISTANCE: 1 hour; 10.1 miles round-trip.

MAPS: Colville National Forest, West Half (G, 4). *Washington Road & Recreation Atlas*, p. 49 (G, 9).

INFORMATION: Colville National Forest's Three Rivers Ranger District.

GETTING THERE: Take S.R. 20 east from Sherman Pass for about 15 miles, or about 7.7 miles west from the junction with U.S. 395. Turn south onto Canyon Creek Road (136), at the sign for Bangs Mountain Scenic Drive, and set your odometer to 0.

REST STOPS: Canyon Creek Campground at the start of the drive.

THE DRIVE: Canyon Creek Road follows its namesake through mixed forest, climbing steadily. About 2.3 miles from the highway is Donaldson Draw, a wooded, rocky and narrow canyon. As a roadside interpretive sign explains, thousands of years ago this region lay beneath ice sheets thousands of feet thick, and the highest peaks in these mountains stood above the ice like islands. When the climate warmed and the ice melted, some 10,000 to 15,000 years ago, torrents of meltwater flowed southward, spilling over ridges and rapidly eroding numerous steep-walled canyons like Donaldson Draw. As the road climbs out of the draw it forks. This is the start of a short loop that bends around the southeastern flank of Bangs Mountain, so you can take either fork. On the return drive you'll have a view down into Donaldson Draw, providing, with some reliance on the imagination, a glimpse back to the time of melting continental ice sheets.

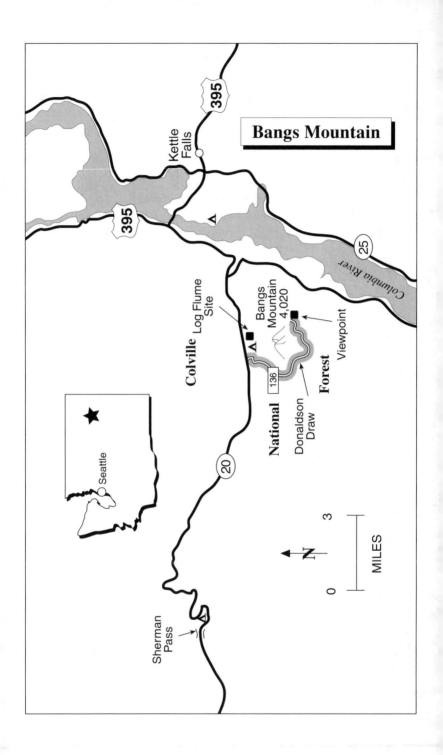

Bangs Mountain

395

Kettle Falls

395

25

Columbia River

Colville Log Flume Site

Bangs Mountain 4,020

Viewpoint

136

Donaldson Draw

National   **Forest**

20

Seattle

★

3

N

MILES

0

Sherman Pass

Bon Ayre Ridge

LOCATION: Selkirk Mountains of northeastern Washington, northeast of Colville. Colville National Forest. Stevens County.

HIGHLIGHTS: This rugged region, on the western flank of the northern Rocky Mountains, was sculpted by great ice sheets that melted away at the end of the last ice age, some 10,000 to 15,000 years ago. The heavily forested and remote terrain, which is affected by both coastal and Rocky Mountain climates, belies the notion that Washington east of the Cascades is only semiarid steppe.

DIFFICULTY: Easy, on good dirt-and-gravel roads. Watch for logging trucks and fallen snags (dead trees). Not all of the road numbers you will encounter are on maps of the area.

TIME & DISTANCE: 1.5 hours; about 23.5 miles.

MAPS: Colville National Forest, East Half (K-M, 3). *Washington Road & Recreation Atlas*, p. 50 (E, 3-4).

INFORMATION: Colville National Forest's Three Rivers Ranger District.

GETTING THERE: From the S.R. 20 & U.S. 395 junction in Colville, take S.R. 20 east a bit more than a mile. Turn left (north) onto Aladdin Road. Follow it for about 13.6 miles. Turn right (east) onto North Fork Mill Creek Road (7015). Set your odometer to 0.

REST STOPS: A scenic ridge-top saddle at mile 11.6 is a great place to pause and gaze across waves of ranges to the east and south.

THE DRIVE: North Fork Mill Creek Road follows the stream through the forest, then crosses it at a tight bend to the right at mile 2.6. Then it climbs gradually through old clearcuts, and makes a number of easy switchbacks as it takes you up to Bon Ayre Ridge, providing views across the valley and hills below, and north into Canada. By mile 8.7 the road narrows to a single lane, and becomes something of a tunnel through a verdant woodland. Just beyond mile 9, as you round Blacktail Butte, you'll reach the highest point on the drive, about 4,900 feet. At mile 11.6 the road bends right (south) and brings you to a saddle about 3,900 feet high, with an expansive view across waves of distant mountains and valleys. At mile 12.7 you will reach Middle Fork Mill Creek Road (county road 4668). Go left. About 3.4 miles farther is Rocky Creek Road (4699). Go right (east) here, toward Tiger Highway (S.R. 20) and Tiger Meadows. From here the road narrows to a somewhat rocky and rutted two-track. Almost 5 miles from where you joined Rocky Creek Road, the route crosses a small bridge and improves considerably. In 2.7 more miles you'll reach S.R. 20, at Tiger Meadows.

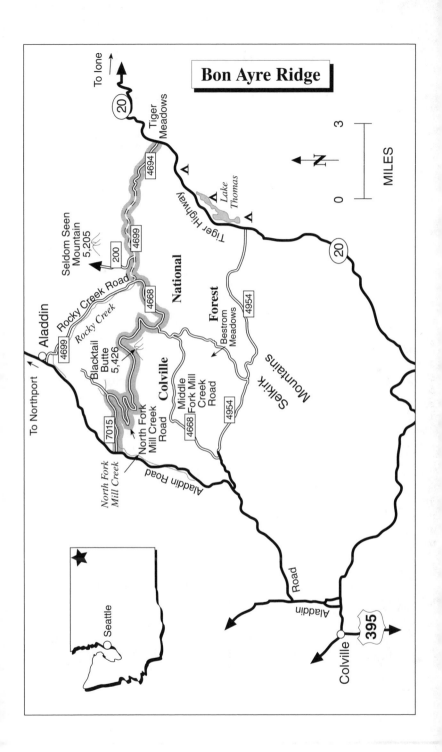

Bon Ayre Ridge

Smackout Pass

LOCATION: Selkirk Mountains of northeastern Washington. West of Ione. Colville National Forest. Pend Oreille County.

HIGHLIGHTS: The Selkirk Mountains, a branch of the northern Rocky Mountains that was shaped by glaciers thousands of years ago (like the rest of northern Washington), belie the image of eastern Washington as one vast, semiarid steppe. This short trip takes you through a rugged, boulder-strewn landscape, providing views of seemingly endless forested mountains and lush, picturesque meadows.

DIFFICULTY: Easy, on a maintained gravel road.

TIME & DISTANCE: 1 hour; 14 miles.

MAPS: Colville National Forest, East Half (L-N, 2). *Washington Road & Recreation Atlas*, p. 50 (C-D, 4-6).

INFORMATION: Colville National Forest's Three Rivers Ranger District.

GETTING THERE: This east-west drive can be taken in either direction. **To go west,** the way I describe: Make your way to Ione, on S.R. 31 along the Pend Oreille River. Take Houghton Street west, across the railroad tracks and past the elementary school. Go left at the stop sign. Drive a block, then turn right, onto Smackout Pass Road. Set your odometer to 0. **To go east:** From Northport, on the Columbia River just south of the Canadian border, take Aladdin Road southeast about 11 miles. Turn left (east) onto Smackout Creek Road.

REST STOPS: No place in particular, but the pass, with its long vistas, is good place to stop for a bit.

THE DRIVE: From Ione, Smackout Pass Road (2714) ascends into high, rolling mountains dotted by outcrops of crystalline granite and blanketed by mixed forest. By mile 7.4, as the road zigzags beneath power lines, you'll see boulders everywhere, a common sight where ice-age glaciers scoured the land, then melted and retreated. At mile 7.6 you're on Smackout Pass (about 3,800 feet). Beyond the pass the road becomes Smackout Creek Road (4708). It makes a long, meandering descent to Smackout Valley and a 400-acre meadow that has been divided into four pastures to demonstrate the conservation value of annual grazing rotation (watch out for cattle in the road). Following Smackout Creek, you will reach paved Aladdin Road several miles later. Colville is to the left (southwest), Northport to the right (northwest).

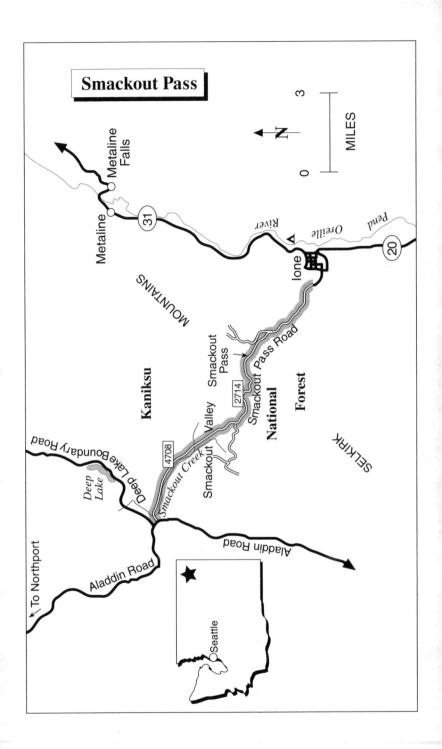

Smackout Pass

Hooknose Ridge

LOCATION: Selkirk Mountains, just south of the Canadian border in Washington's far northeastern corner. Colville National Forest. Stevens and Pend Oreille counties.

HIGHLIGHTS: This backway winds through an intriguing expanse of forest scored by ridges and canyons. At the eastern end, you can tour an underground cave (Crawford State Park/Gardner Cave), and take a short forest hike from there to the U.S./Canada border.

DIFFICULTY: Easy, on a gravel and native-surface mountain road. The hike to the border is easy as well.

TIME & DISTANCE: 45 minutes (excluding Gardner Cave and the hike to the international border); 16.3 miles. The hike is about a quarter-mile.

MAPS: Colville National Forest, East Half (M-N, 1). *Washington Road & Recreation Atlas*, p. 50 (A, 5-6).

INFORMATION: Colville National Forest's Sullivan Lake Ranger District.

GETTING THERE: To go east (the direction I describe): Get to Northport, on S.R. 25 and the Columbia River near the Canadian border. Continue north along the river, on Boundary Highway. Shortly before the border curve eastward, on Deep Lake-Boundary Road. About 1.6 miles from where the road bends south, turn left (east) onto Cedar Creek Road, and set your odometer to 0. **To go west:** Take S.R. 31 to Metaline. Just north of town, turn left (northwest) onto Boundary Road (2975), and head to Crawford State Park/Gardner Cave. Where the road into the park angles right, continue ahead, onto road 6270.

REST STOPS: Take the tour of Crawford State Park's Gardner Cave, and the hike to the international border, marked by a logged east-west swath. The park has tables, toilets and water.

THE DRIVE: Cedar Creek Road (county road 4752/forest road 6270) begins as graded gravel through picturesque meadows and rangelands. After about 5 miles, as it enters the national forest, it diminishes to a typical single-lane forest road. Then, as it climbs toward Hooknose Ridge, it dwindles even further to a mere two-track road pinched between a drop-off into a canyon on the left and a moss-covered cliff on the right. Soon the forest will close in around you, creating a tunnel-like passageway. After crossing the ridge, while still deep in the forest, you will pass a roadside mining claim. Beyond that begins a long, steady descent. About 16.3 miles from Deep Lake-Boundary Road the dirt road will end, and you will see the entrance to Crawford State Park on your left. From here, paved Boundary Road will take you to S.R. 31 near the quaint town of Metaline Falls, which is worth a visit.

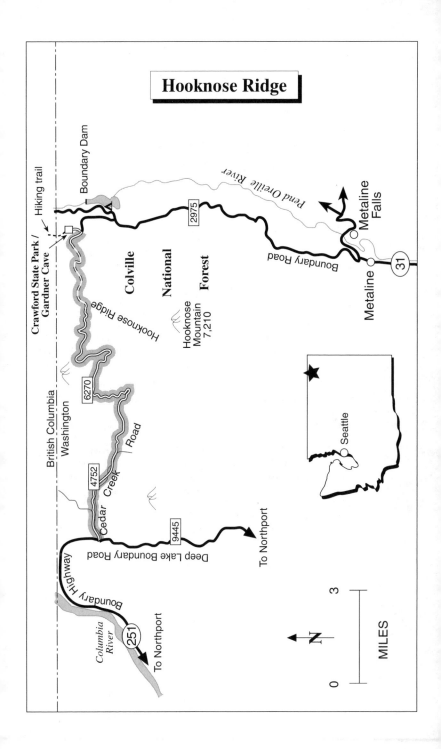

Hooknose Ridge

Highland Loop-Pingston Crk.

LOCATION: In the hills north and east of Kettle Falls, on the Columbia River in northeastern Washington. Stevens County.

HIGHLIGHTS: These pastoral country roads in the hills above the Columbia River will take you through bucolic pastures and stands of pine and aspen, and past old farms and gold mines. This isn't an adventurous trip, just a very pretty one that provides great views of Colville Valley.

DIFFICULTY: Easy, on well-maintained gravel roads.

TIME & DISTANCE: A half-hour; 10.8 miles.

MAPS: *Washington Road & Recreation Atlas*, p. 49 (F, 10-11). Colville National Forest, West Half (H-J, 3-4).

INFORMATION: Stevens County.

GETTING THERE: This route makes a semi-loop, so you can go either way. To go the way I describe, take U.S. 395 east for 3.5 miles from the only traffic light in Kettle Falls. Turn left (north) onto Highland Loop Road, then set your odometer to 0. Or, take S.R. 25 north for 3.6 miles from the junction with U.S. 395, and turn right (east) onto Pingston Creek Road.

REST STOPS: There aren't any, and you won't need one.

THE DRIVE: Highland Loop Road climbs steeply from U.S. 395, into rolling, golden-brown and very picturesque hills that provide terrific views of Colville Valley. Then the winding little road enters mixed woodland, and arrives at Pingston Creek Road about 2.5 miles from the highway. Go right, and follow Pingston Creek Road through the forest on Echo Mountain. Soon you'll be making a long, steady descent toward the Columbia River. A half mile after the road passes below a railroad trestle, you will reach S.R. 25 and the end of the drive. Kettle Falls is to the left.

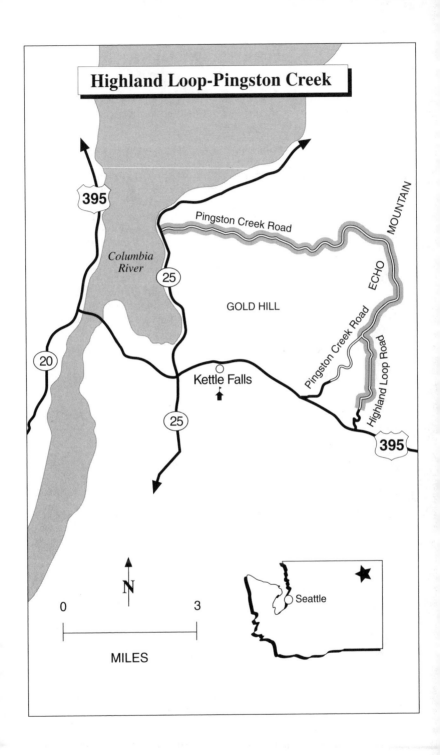

Highland Loop-Pingston Creek

395

Columbia River

25

Pingston Creek Road

GOLD HILL

ECHO MOUNTAIN

Pingston Creek Road

Highland Loop Road

20

Kettle Falls

25

395

N

0   3

MILES

Seattle

Salmo Mountain

LOCATION: Selkirk Mountains, near the Canadian and Idaho borders in Washington's far northeastern corner. Colville National Forest. Pend Oreille County.

HIGHLIGHTS: Few of Washington's mountain roads will make you feel more like you're traveling through an unspoiled wildland than the roads to remote 6,828-foot Salmo Mountain. The route is flanked by the rugged Salmo-Priest Wilderness, which protects stands of old-growth western red cedar, Douglas fir and western hemlock, species commonly associated with western Washington's dense forests, as well as endangered grizzly bear and woodland caribou. Salmo Mountain, topped by a lookout tower, stands at the edge of the wilderness, and provides a spectacular vista. You can combine this drive with Pass Creek Pass (Tour 28).

DIFFICULTY: Easy, on maintained dirt-and-gravel until you reach road 270, the final segment. While still easy with high clearance and 2WD, the road is primitive, with a rougher native surface.

TIME & DISTANCE: 2 hours; 42.5 miles round-trip.

MAPS: Colville National Forest, East Half (P-R, 1-2). *Washington Road & Recreation Atlas*, p. 51 (A-C, 7-9).

INFORMATION: Colville National Forest's Sullivan Lake Ranger District, on the northwest shore of the lake.

GETTING THERE: From Metaline Falls, take S.R. 31 north about 1.3 miles. Turn right (south) onto Sullivan Lake Road, and drive toward Sullivan Lake. At the north end of the lake turn east onto road 22 (Sullivan Creek Road). Set your odometer to 0 there.

REST STOPS: There are campgrounds at Sullivan Lake, and primitive campsites and vault toilets along Sullivan Creek, popular for fishing. The lookout is proposed for addition to the Forest Service's cabin rental system.

THE DRIVE: Road 22, paved for a half mile, follows Sullivan Creek east and north up a forested valley flanked by legally designated wilderness. At 6 miles from Sullivan Lake, road 22 branches to the southeast, toward Idaho (Tour 28). From here, the road to Salmo Mountain is No. 2220. About 6 miles from the junction the road begins its ascent toward Salmo Pass, and eventually traverses a shelf from which you can gaze across the glaciated Selkirks. At Salmo Pass, about 19 miles from Sullivan Lake, turn left (north) onto road 270. This road ascends to the lookout in 2.3 miles. Climb the stairs to the platform for an inspiring view. Canada is only 2 miles north, and Idaho 3 miles east.

ALSO TRY: Roads 2212 and 245 to the top of 6,483-foot Sullivan Mountain, for another fine view of this wild and remote region.

SALMO MOUNTAIN

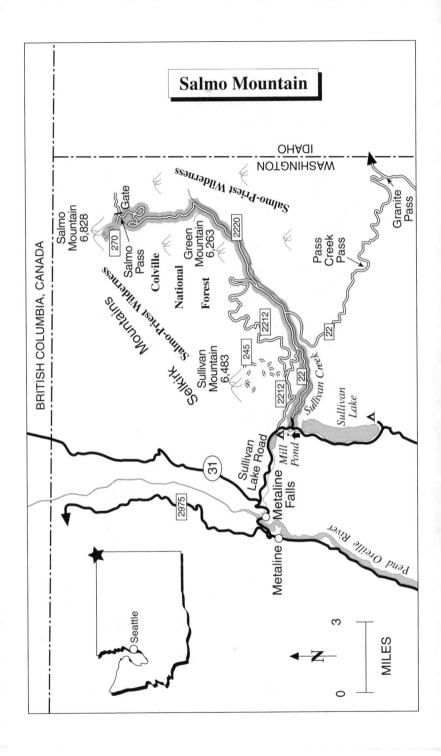

Salmo Mountain

Salmo Mountain (Tour 27)

Cascade River Road (Tour 31)

Pass Creek Pass

LOCATION: Selkirk Mountains, near the Canadian and Idaho borders in Washington's far northeastern corner. Colville National Forest and Kaniksu National Forest (administered as Idaho Panhandle National Forests). Pend Oreille County.

HIGHLIGHTS: The serpentine little road from Sullivan Lake to Granite Pass climbs the impressive canyon of Pass Creek. Then it crosses Pass Creek Pass (5,580 feet) at the southern tip of Salmo-Priest Wilderness, and provides spectacular views across the mountain ranges of northern Idaho as it descends toward Idaho's sparkling Priest Lake. This drive can be combined with Tour 27, Salmo Mountain.

DIFFICULTY: Easy, on a good dirt-and-gravel road, but there are many blind curves.

TIME & DISTANCE: 1 hour; 21 miles from Sullivan Lake to Granite Pass, the end of the trip. It's another 14 miles to Nordman, Idaho, and 50 miles to Priest River, Idaho.

MAPS: Colville National Forest, East Half (P-R, 2). *Washington Road & Recreation Atlas*, p. 51 (C-D, 7-9).

INFORMATION: Colville National Forest's Sullivan Lake Ranger District, on the northwest shore of the lake. Idaho Panhandle National Forests' Priest Lake Ranger District.

GETTING THERE: From Metaline Falls, take S.R. 31 north about 1.3 miles. Turn right (south) onto Old Sullivan Lake Road, and drive toward Sullivan Lake. At the north end of the lake turn east onto road 22 (Sullivan Creek Road). Set your odometer to 0 there. In 6 miles turn right (southeast), toward Priest Lake.

REST STOPS: There are campgrounds at Sullivan Lake. Stagger Inn Campground, Granite Falls and Roosevelt Grove of Ancient Cedars are 1.7 miles south of Granite Pass.

THE DRIVE: At the junction of roads 2220 (to Salmo Mountain, Tour 27) and 22, turn right (south) and follow 22 as it winds along Pass Creek toward Pass Creek Pass and Idaho. Here you will no doubt feel a genuine sense of remoteness, for as far as you can see are waves of rugged, deeply furrowed mountain ranges. At Pass Creek Pass the road enters Kaniksu National Forest, part of Idaho Panhandle National Forests, and its number changes to 302. The magnificent mountain vistas continue on the 7-mile descent to 3,760-foot Granite Pass, where road 302, now much-improved compared to what you've been on, bends southeast toward Idaho.

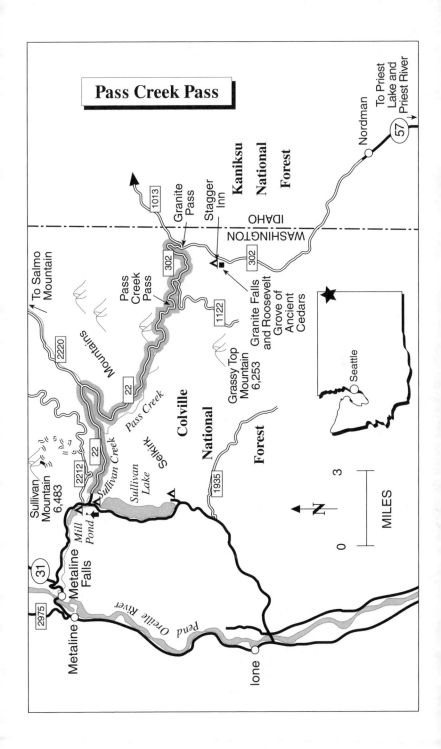

Pass Creek Pass

Kaniksu National Forest

Nordman

To Priest Lake and Priest River

57

1013
Granite Pass
Stagger Inn

IDAHO
WASHINGTON

302

302

1122

Granite Falls and Roosevelt Grove of Ancient Cedars

To Salmo Mountain

2220

Pass Creek Pass

Mountains

22

Selkirk

Grassy Top Mountain 6,253

Colville National

Pass Creek

Forest

1935

Sullivan Creek

22

2212

Sullivan Lake

Seattle

3

MILES

0

N

Sullivan Mountain 6,483

Mill Pond

31

Metaline Falls

2975

Metaline

Pend Oreille River

Ione

87

Ruby Loop

LOCATION: North-central Washington, south of Conconully and northwest of Okanogan. Okanogan County.

HIGHLIGHTS: The foothills east of the Cascade Range occupy a transition zone, where dry, rolling, nearly treeless steppes meet the vast conifer forests of the well-watered western side of the state. The silver mines that spawned the late 19th-century boom-town of Ruby have long been idle, but the rugged landscape remains a mix of high ridges, steep canyons, grassy meadows, and stands of aspen that promise late-summer or early-autumn color. Rubble piles, water-filled pits, and rocky little roads that are quite different from the logging roads one finds elsewhere in the state are about all that remain of the region's mining legacy.

DIFFICULTY: Easy, with some steep, narrow and rocky segments that will require high clearance if not 4WD. **Note:** Old mine sites are dangerous; use caution.

TIME & DISTANCE: 3 hours; about 30 miles.

MAP: Okanogan National Forest (L-M, 4-6).

INFORMATION: Bureau of Land Management's Wenatchee Field Office.

GETTING THERE: From Okanogan, take S.R. 20 west for about 9 miles, toward Loup Loup Summit. Turn north onto Bawlf Road/Buzzard Lake Road (2065) at milepost 224. Set your odometer to 0.

REST STOPS: Rock Creek Campground.

THE DRIVE: It's about 4.5 miles to Buzzard Lake, where you'll find stands of aspen. At the lake, pass the turn to the right (east), and continue north. A half-mile north of the lake is a Y. Keep left, and the road, now rocky and steep, will climb toward Arlington Ridge. About 1.8 miles from the lake is another junction. Go left, toward Ruby Hill. About 3 miles farther you will be on Arlington Ridge. Here the road (now Arlington Ridge Road) bends left, and makes a rocky 3.6-mile descent along the ridge's west side, passing more mine sites before reaching Loup Loup Canyon Road (2045). You'll take Loup Loup Canyon Road south later. For now, go right (north) for a half mile to a T-junction. Go right again, and descend on the steep one-lane road for 1.2 miles, to Salmon Creek Road. This is the site of Ruby. Founded in 1886, it was named for the nearby Ruby Mine, which was named for a creek where miners found what they thought were rubies. Ruby died in 1893 when the price of silver plunged. Only a few foundations remain, hidden by brush. Return to Loup Loup Canyon Road, and follow it south past the turn to Arlington Ridge and into a rock-walled canyon that also was the site of a mining camp that fell victim to the silver bust. About 2.2 miles from the turn to Arlington Ridge, granite China Wall is on the left. Built in 1889, the wall is a relic of Arlington Mill, which fell into bankruptcy before construction

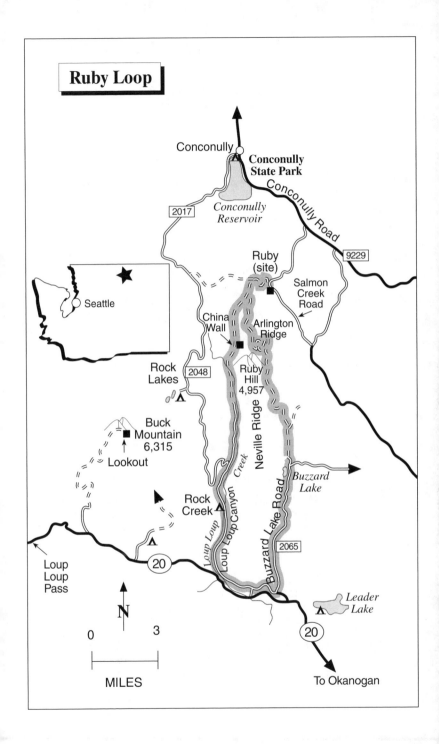

Ruby Loop

Conconully

Conconully State Park

Conconully Road

2017

Conconully Reservoir

9229

Ruby (site)

Salmon Creek Road

China Wall

Arlington Ridge

Seattle

Rock Lakes

2048

Ruby Hill 4,957

Buck Mountain 6,315

Lookout

Neville Ridge

Creek

Rock Creek

Loup Loup

Loup Loup Canyon

Buzzard Lake Road

Buzzard Lake

Loup Loup Pass

20

2065

Leader Lake

N

0   3

MILES

20

To Okanogan

was completed. In another 4.6 miles you'll come to Rock Creek Campground. S.R. 20 is 4 miles beyond that.

Buck Mountain Lookout

LOCATION: North-central Washington, west of Okanogan, north of S.R. 20. Okanogan National Forest. Okanogan County.

HIGHLIGHTS: This short but immensely rewarding side trip off S.R. 20 takes you to a 6,135-foot peak on the eastern slope of the Cascade Range. The views of the region where Washington's dry eastern expanse meets the forested mountains is outstanding. But of course, as with all lookout sites, the best views are from the summit, where the state maintains a 20-foot-tall lookout for emergency use. Unfortunately, access to the tower, built in 1961, is restricted to Washington Department of Natural Resources personnel.

DIFFICULTY: This is an easy-to-moderate 4WD route, although it becomes fairly rough, steep and narrow along the final 1.5 miles or so. I recommend using low-range 4WD. There is one tight switchback that you may have to take in two moves.

TIME & DISTANCE: 1 hour; 11.6 miles round-trip.

MAP: Okanogan National Forest (K-L, 5).

INFORMATION: Washington Department of Natural Resources. Okanogan National Forest's Methow Valley Ranger District.

GETTING THERE: From Okanogan, take S.R. 20 west for about 15.3 miles, toward Loup Loup Summit. Before reaching the summit, turn north onto Buck Mountain Road (an easy turn to miss) and set the odometer to 0.

REST STOPS: The summit.

THE DRIVE: The little two-track road begins climbing immediately through state forest land, leaving little doubt why Buck Mountain was developed as a lookout site in 1919. By mile 3.5 you're getting terrific views down forested foothills to the vast, treeless expanses that characterize so much of eastern Washington. When you reach a small clearing, a flat spot with twin pines, keep right. From there the road becomes a mountainside shelf, and passes through a large stand of aspen. Keep right again when you reach a tree with a large boulder beside it. The road is steep, rough and narrow here, so if you want to take in the spectacular view spreading out before you, stop. About 5.8 miles from the highway you'll encounter a couple of switchbacks, the second of which is quite tight. Just beyond it is a small parking area. From there, just hike the rocky footpath a short distance to the nearby lookout tower.

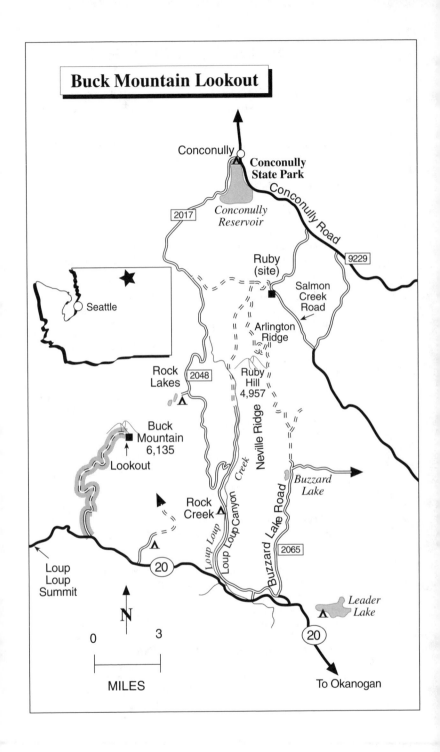

Buck Mountain Lookout

Conconully

Conconully State Park

Conconully Road

2017

Conconully Reservoir

Seattle

Ruby (site)

9229

Salmon Creek Road

Arlington Ridge

Rock Lakes

2048

Ruby Hill 4,957

Neville Ridge

Buck Mountain 6,135

Lookout

Rock Creek

Loup Loup Canyon

Creek

Loup Loup

Buzzard Lake Road

Buzzard Lake

Loup Loup Summit

20

2065

N

0 3

MILES

Leader Lake

20

To Okanogan

91

Cascade River Road

LOCATION: Southeast of Marblemount. Mt. Baker-Snoqualmie National Forest and North Cascades National Park (South Unit). Skagit County.

HIGHLIGHTS: Cascade River Road ascends a forested valley hewn by glaciers and long traveled by Indians, pioneers, explorers and miners. Today, this remote entrance to North Cascades National Park attracts visitors headed for Cascade Pass (5,384 feet) and views of waterfalls, alpine meadows, craggy peaks, glaciers and snowfields. Its nearby namesake is a federally designated wild and scenic river.

DIFFICULTY: Easy. The first 7 miles are paved. The remainder is mostly maintained gravel and dirt. The hike to Cascade Pass, which climbs 1,800 feet, is considered moderate.

TIME & DISTANCE: 1.5 hours and 24 miles, one way. From the trailhead at road's end, the hike to Cascade Pass is about 5 hours and 7.4 miles round-trip.

MAPS: Mt. Baker-Snoqualmie National Forest (G-K, 4-5). *Washington Road & Recreation Atlas*, pp. 43 (G-H, 10-12) & 44 (G-H, 1-3).

INFORMATION: Mt. Baker-Snoqualmie National Forest's Mt. Baker Ranger District. North Cascades National Park, which has a wilderness information center north of S.R. 20 west of Marblemount.

GETTING THERE: Take S.R. 20 to Marblemount, west of the park's midsection. Drive east from S.R. 20 on Cascade River Road, crossing the bridge over the Skagit River, where you can set your odometer to 0.

REST STOPS: There are two Forest Service campgrounds along the way. You'll find tables and toilets at the trailhead. You will need a Northwest Forest Pass to park.

THE DRIVE: Once across the Skagit River, you will see the smaller Cascade River coursing down the valley that leads into the mountains ahead. At mile 6.7 the road enters the national forest, where a pullout offers a terrific view of glacial and geologic handiwork. The pavement ends a short distance farther. From there, you will meander below a thick forest canopy. Soon the road passes Marble Creek and Mineral Park campgrounds. 0.6 mile beyond the park boundary, a spur branches left. It goes a short distance to a gorgeous cedar-shaded picnic area beside the North Fork of the Cascade River. The main road climbs to another viewpoint north of Glacier Peak Wilderness, an inspiring sight. At road's end you can park and gaze out at an imposing landscape where, it seems, the last ice age hasn't ended.

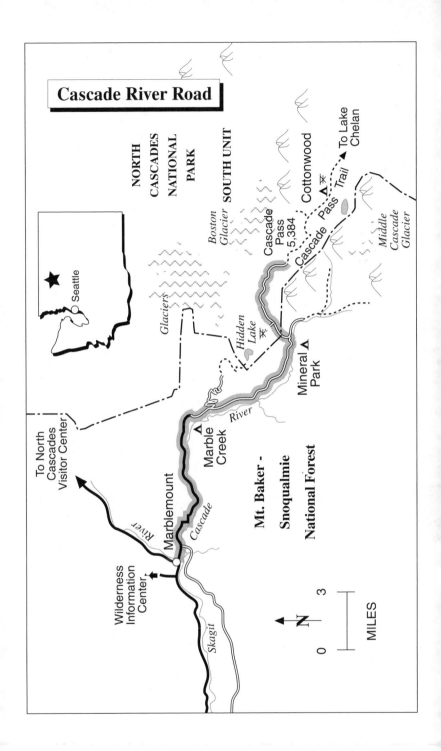

93

Mountain Loop Highway

LOCATION: Western side of the North Cascades. Mt. Baker-Snoqualmie National Forest. Between Darrington and Granite Falls. Snohomish County.

HIGHLIGHTS: From the old railroad town of Granite Falls to the logging center of Darrington, Mountain Loop Highway (a Forest Service scenic byway) follows the Stillaguamish and Sauk rivers through a mountainous region that blends soaring glaciated peaks, steep valleys, waterfalls, ice caves, even the ghost town of Monte Cristo. Don't miss the beautiful foot trail to Big Four Ice Caves, snowfield tunnels formed by meltwater and the flow of warm air.

DIFFICULTY: Easy. Suited to low-clearance 2WD vehicles. Road surfaces range from two-lane asphalt to single-lane gravel. About 14 miles are unpaved. The easy walking and biking trail to Monte Cristo follows the grade of the old Everett & Monte Cristo Railroad. The trail to Big Four Ice Caves is easy.

TIME & DISTANCE: 2.5 hours; 54 miles. Hiking trails, viewpoints and historic sites warrant taking a full day. The trail to Monte Cristo is 8 miles, round-trip. Big Four Ice Caves trail is 2 miles, round-trip. Trailhead parking requires a Northwest Forest Pass.

MAPS: Mt. Baker-Snoqualmie National Forest, North Half (C-G, 6-8). *Washington Road & Recreation Atlas*, pp. 56-57 (C-F, 5-11).

INFORMATION: Mt. Baker-Snoqualmie National Forest's Darrington Ranger Station. Verlot Public Service Center, in Verlot.

GETTING THERE: You can begin at Granite Falls or Darrington. **To begin at Granite Falls:** From S.R. 9 east of Everett, take S.R. 92 northeast to Granite Falls. Turn north on Mountain Loop Highway (S.R. 92/forest road 20). **To begin at Darrington:** Take S.R. 530 northeast to Darrington from S.R. 9 at Arlington. In the center of Darrington, turn south on Sauk Avenue, then east on Darrington Street. The latter will bend southeast and become Darrington-Clear Creek Road, which becomes Mountain Loop Highway.

REST STOPS: There are many places to camp (including Monte Cristo), gaze at the mountains or have a picnic. Refer to your map.

THE DRIVE: Skirting three wilderness areas, this trip winds through two river valleys noted for mining, logging, sightseeing and seemingly boundless outdoor recreation. The views of the mountains are spectacular east of Granite Falls, while south of Darrington the lush forest forms an arboreal tunnel. About 25.5 miles east of Granite Falls (or 14.5 miles east of the Verlot Public Service Center) is Big Four Picnic Area, and the very good (and popular) trail to Big Four Ice Caves and waterfall, at the base of 6,135-foot Big Four Mountain. (The caves are dangerous; view them from a distance). At 2,361-foot Barlow Pass,

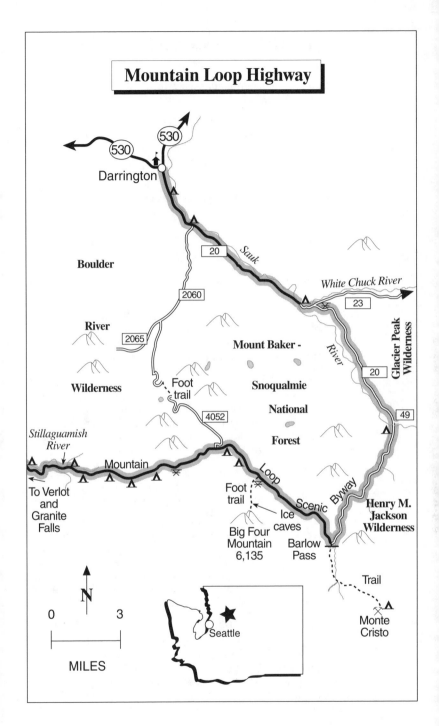

Mountain Loop Highway

530

530

Darrington

20

Sauk

Boulder

White Chuck River

2060

23

River

River

2065

20

Mount Baker -

Glacier Peak Wilderness

Wilderness

Foot trail

Snoqualmie

4052

National

49

Stillaguamish River

Forest

Mountain

Loop

To Verlot and Granite Falls

Foot trail

Big Four Mountain 6,135

Ice caves

Scenic

Byway

Henry M. Jackson Wilderness

Barlow Pass

N

Trail

0   3

Monte Cristo

Seattle

MILES

the road's unpaved section (often closed in winter) either begins or ends, depending on your direction of travel. At the pass is the trail to Monte Cristo, a ghost town from the late 19th and early 20th centuries.

Shady Pass-Lake Chelan

LOCATION: Chelan Mountains, between Entiat River Road and Lake Chelan. Wenatchee National Forest. Chelan County.

HIGHLIGHTS: Traversing the rugged and steep Chelan Mountains provides excellent views, from over 6,000 feet elevation, of the Cascade Range, Entiat Valley, Lake Chelan, and the Columbia Basin to the southeast. The burned forest you'll encounter is an eerie sight.

DIFFICULTY: Easy, on a high-clearance native-surface road.

TIME & DISTANCE: 26 miles; 1.5-2 hours.

MAPS: Wenatchee National Forest, North Half (H-L, 5-6). *Washington Road & Recreation Atlas*, p. 59 (F-G, 8-11).

INFORMATION: Wenatchee National Forest's Entiat and Chelan districts.

GETTING THERE: To end at Lake Chelan (the way I describe): From Entiat, on U.S. 97, take Entiat River Road (S.R. 51) north for 29 miles. Turn right (east) onto road 5900. Set the odometer to 0. **To begin at Lake Chelan:** Take the western leg of U.S. 97 about 3 miles west of Chelan. Turn right (north) onto South Lakeshore Road. Drive north along Lake Chelan for 15 miles, to Twentyfive Mile Creek State Park. Instead of turning into the lakeside park, continue to road 5900. Take 5900, which is paved at the outset, toward Grouse Mountain Campground. The pavement will end at the junction with Stormy Mountain Road (8410) to Slide Ridge (Tour 34).

REST STOPS: Junior Point, Handy Spring, Grouse Mountain, Snowberry Bowl campgrounds. There also are campgrounds on the Entiat River, and at Twentyfive Mile Creek State Park.

THE DRIVE: Road 5900 winds steeply up the side of the canyon where Lake Creek meanders down to the Entiat River. As the road ascends 3,700 feet in less than 8 miles, to a ridge, you will have expanding views of the Entiat Valley and the Cascades. By mile 8.5 you're at Shady Pass, at the junction with road 112. Stay on 5900. Here begins a long stretch of shelf road, high above a deep valley. In another 4.3 miles is a T-junction. The trip goes left, toward Lake Chelan. The spur to the right goes to Handy Spring Campground, the Devil's Backbone hiking trailhead and excellent views of the region. Road 5900 soon reaches the turnoff for Junior Point CG, where you'll find an inspiring 360-degree panorama from 6,654 feet. From there, road 5900 crosses Chesapeake Saddle, then narrows to a shelf again and passes through a burned area. Eventually you will arrive at Grouse Mountain Campground, then descend toward Lake Chelan, reaching pavement in 5.5 miles at the junction with Stormy Mountain Road (8410). Twentyfive Mile Creek State Park is a short distance ahead.

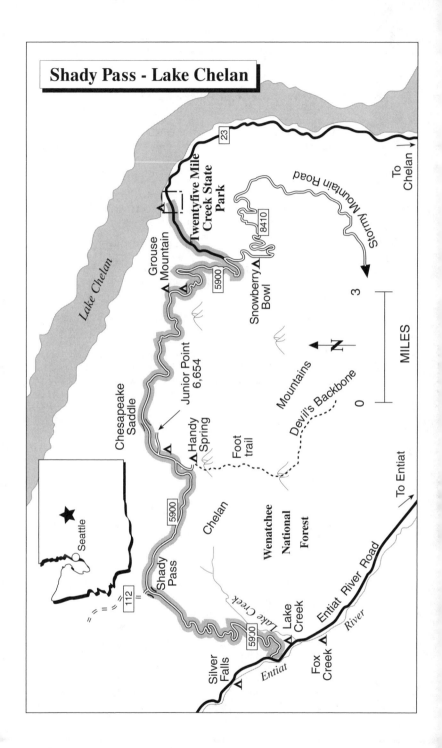

Shady Pass - Lake Chelan

Lake Chelan

Twentyfive Mile Creek State Park

Grouse Mountain

Chesapeake Saddle

Junior Point 6,654

Handy Spring

Shady Pass

Silver Falls

Snowberry Bowl

8410

Stormy Mountain Road

To Chelan

N

MILES

0   3

Mountains

Devil's Backbone

Foot trail

Chelan

Wenatchee National Forest

To Entiat

Lake Creek

Entiat River Road

Entiat River

Lake Creek

Fox Creek

Seattle

5900

5900

5900

112

23

Stormy Mountain Road

LOCATION: Chelan Mountains, between Entiat River Road and Lake Chelan. Wenatchee National Forest. Chelan County.

HIGHLIGHTS: After climbing 4,000 feet, much of it on narrow mountainside shelves with long drop-offs, you will follow a ridge with panoramas that reach from the peaks of the Cascades to Lake Chelan and the vast, semiarid Columbia Basin to the east.

DIFFICULTY: Easy, on a largely narrow, high-clearance and often rocky mountain road. You may encounter rocks, deadfall and washouts due to wildfire damage.

TIME & DISTANCE: 2 hours; 36 miles.

MAPS: Wenatchee National Forest, North Half (K-L, 6-8). *Washington Road & Recreation Atlas*, pp. 59 (G-H, 10-11) & 73 (A-B, 10-11).

INFORMATION: Wenatchee National Forest's Entiat and Chelan ranger districts.

GETTING THERE: To begin at Lake Chelan, the way I describe: Take the western leg of U.S. 97 about 3 miles west of Chelan. Turn right (northwest) onto South Lakeshore Road. Drive north along Lake Chelan for 15 miles, to Twentyfive Mile Creek State Park. Instead of turning into the park, continue to road 5900. Take 5900 to the junction with Stormy Mountain Road (8410), which will be on your left where the pavement ends. Go through the gate, and drive toward Ramona Park and Snowberry Bowl Campground. **To end at Lake Chelan:** From Entiat, take Entiat River Road north about 11.2 miles. Turn right (east) onto Mud Creek Road (5300).

REST STOPS: Twentyfive Mile Creek State Park has camping, boating, fishing and a small store. Along the way are Snowberry Bowl and Windy Camp campgrounds.

THE DRIVE: Stormy Mountain Road, named for a peak about midway along the drive, first descends into the canyon of Twentyfive Mile Creek. Then it crosses the creek and makes a long, serpentine climb, providing terrific views of Lake Chelan and the Chelan Mountains. About 7.6 miles into the drive you will be on top of Slide Ridge, above 4,500 feet elevation. From here, follow the ridgecrest south, meandering from one side of it to the other, enjoying outstanding panoramic views along almost every mile. After about 14 miles the road will take you through a burned area, where brilliant wildflowers and other plants now sprout amid charred dead trees, called snags. Beyond that is the turn for Windy Camp. About 1.2 miles farther the road crosses a saddle, where, from almost 6,000 feet elevation, you will have a dizzying view across endless mountains and canyons to the northwest. If that's not enough beauty, another such view awaits at another saddle a mile ahead. Then the road begins a long descent. Continue past the turn for road 5380, and follow road 8410 to Mud Creek Road (5300; Tour 35). Go right (southwest) to Entiat River Road.

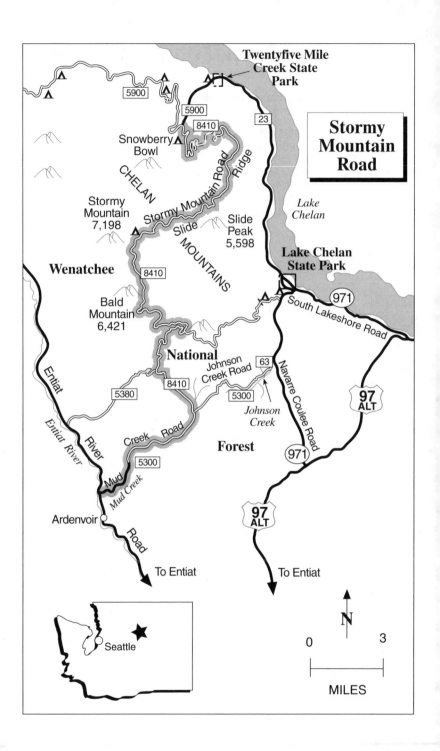

Twentyfive Mile
Creek State
Park

5900

5900

8410

23

Stormy
Mountain
Road

Snowberry
Bowl

CHELAN

*Lake
Chelan*

Stormy
Mountain
7,198

Stormy Mountain Road

Slide

Ridge

Slide
Peak
5,598

Lake Chelan
State Park

Wenatchee

8410

MOUNTAINS

Bald
Mountain
6,421

971

South Lakeshore Road

National

Johnson
Creek Road

63

Entiat

8410

5380

5300

*Johnson
Creek*

Navarre Coulee Road

97
ALT

Creek Road

Forest

971

Entiat River

River

5300

Mud

Mud Creek

97
ALT

Ardenvoir

Road

To Entiat

To Entiat

N

Seattle

0   3

MILES

Mud Creek-Johnson Creek

LOCATION: Chelan Mountains, west of Lake Chelan and northeast of Ardenvoir. Wenatchee National Forest. Chelan County.

HIGHLIGHTS: Forest road 5300 passes through two rocky canyons, with the one along Johnson Creek Road being particularly beautiful. The northeastern end of Johnson Creek Road is a high and narrow canyonside road with a long drop-off. Mud Creek Road passes through an area that burned in the summer of 2001, which, while perhaps not a highlight in the usual sense, is an interesting sight nonetheless.

DIFFICULTY: Easy, on roads that range from low-clearance gravel to high-clearance dirt. A narrow shelf segment of Johnson Creek Road has numerous blind curves and a long drop-off.

TIME & DISTANCE: 11 miles; 45 minutes.

MAPS: Wenatchee National Forest, North Half (J-L, 7-8); *Washington Road & Recreation Atlas*, p. 73 (A-B, 10-12).

INFORMATION: Wenatchee National Forest's Entiat Ranger District.

GETTING THERE: From Entiat (the way I describe): Take Entiat River Road northwest to Ardenvoir. About 1.2 miles north of Ardenvoir, turn right (east) onto Mud Creek Road (5300). Set your odometer to 0. **From Lake Chelan:** Take S.R. 971 (Navarre Coulee Road) south for about 4 miles. Turn right at a residence, onto Johnson Creek Road (5300/county road 63).

REST STOPS: Nowhere in particular.

THE DRIVE: Mud Creek Road is paved for the first 2.5 miles as it meanders along Mud Creek, climbing gradually into rounded hills forested with the ghostly stalks of trees that burned in 2001. About 5.8 miles from Entiat River Road you will pass Stormy Mountain Road (8410) to Slide Ridge (Tour 34). A couple of miles farther the road descends into a ravine, then switchbacks out. When you reach a junction with a road coming in from private property on the right, keep left. From here you will follow Johnson Creek past stands of charred cottonwood. About a mile farther you will enter a narrow rock canyon, where the odds of encountering rockfall are good. Just beyond that the road narrows to a high, and perhaps hair-raising, ledge with few places to pull over and let uphill traffic (which has the right of way) pass. Be careful on the blind curves. Go slow as you pass the residence at the bottom of this steep grade, which ends at S.R. 971. Lake Chelan is left (north).

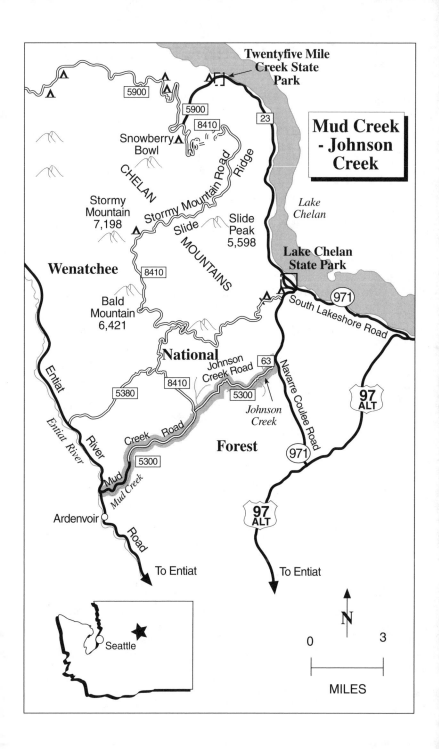

Mud Creek - Johnson Creek

Twentyfive Mile Creek State Park

5900

5900

8410

Snowberry Bowl

CHELAN

Lake Chelan

Stormy Mountain Road

Ridge

Stormy Mountain 7,198

Slide

Slide Peak 5,598

MOUNTAINS

Lake Chelan State Park

8410

Wenatchee

Bald Mountain 6,421

971

South Lakeshore Road

National

Johnson Creek Road

63

8410

5380

5300

Johnson Creek

Navarre Coulee Road

Entiat

Forest

971

Creek Road

Mud Creek

5300

Entiat River

River

97 ALT

Ardenvoir

Road

To Entiat

97 ALT

To Entiat

Seattle

N

0   3

MILES

101

Grade Creek-Cooper Ridge

LOCATION: In the mountains immediately east of Lake Chelan. Wenatchee National Forest. Chelan County.

HIGHLIGHTS: You will climb 4,700 feet up the western face of steep and deeply furrowed mountains that tower over the 55-mile-long, water-filled glacial trough of Lake Chelan. Then you will drive on the crest of the narrow ridge that separates the lake and Methow Valley. Along the way are vistas that stretch from the eastern steppes to the North Cascades.

DIFFICULTY: Easy, on native-surface and gravel roads with narrow and steep sections and long drop-offs.

TIME & DISTANCE: 3.5-4 hours; 59 miles.

MAPS: Wenatchee National Forest, North Half (K-M, 5). *Washington Road & Recreation Atlas* pp. 59 (E-G, 10-12) & 60 (E-G, 1-2).

INFORMATION: Wenatchee National Forest's Chelan Ranger District.

GETTING THERE: Make your way to the town of Chelan, then take S.R. 150 northwest toward Manson. About 2 miles before Manson, turn right (north) onto Wapato Lake Road, at the sign for Wapato and Antilon lakes and Grade Creek. Take Wapato Lake Road to Upper Joe Creek Road, which leads to Grade Creek Road (8200) and the turn for Antilon Lake and South Navarre Campground (see The Drive, below). Set your odometer to 0 there.

REST STOPS: Cooper Mountain, with its nearly 360-degree panorama of this mountainous region, is hard to beat. South Navarre Campground is at the northern tip of the loop.

THE DRIVE: At the turnoff for Antilon Lake, you have two options: Go left, and follow 8200 past Antilon Lake and on through the canyons and ravines that incise the steep, west-facing slopes above Lake Chelan. South Navarre Campground is about 26 miles, and Sawtooth Ridge is another 11. The other option is to climb to Cooper Ridge via road 8210. Each way is rewarding. Either way, you will connect to road 8020, which zigzags along the narrow ridge that is the boundary between Okanogan and Wenatchee national forests. Along the way, especially near the northern end, are some narrow segments with drop-offs. At the south end of the ridge, don't miss the spur to the 5,867-foot summit of Cooper Mountain. From the ridge, two roads—manicured 4010 and more rudimentary 600—descend eastward to Methow Valley. I think 600, and then road 4330, is the more scenic route.

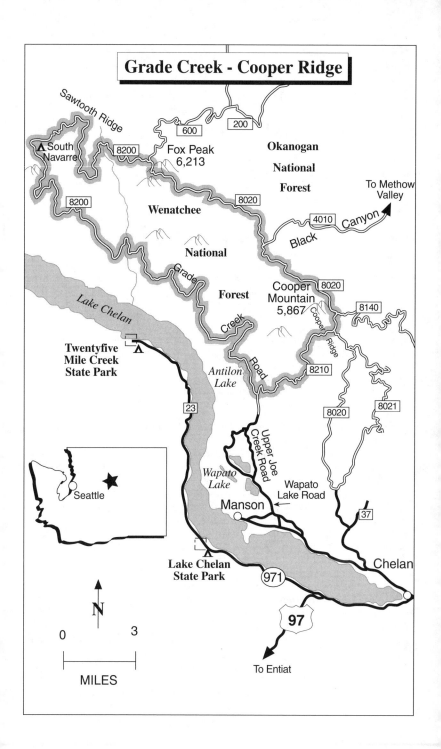

Grade Creek - Cooper Ridge

600
200

South Navarre
8200
Fox Peak
6,213

Okanogan

National

Forest

To Methow Valley

Sawtooth Ridge

8200

8020

Wenatchee

4010
Black Canyon

National

Grade

Cooper Mountain
5,867
8020

8140

Forest

Creek

Cooper Ridge

Lake Chelan

Twentyfive Mile Creek State Park

Antilon Lake

Road

8210

8020
8021

23

Upper Joe Creek Road

Wapato Lake

Wapato Lake Road

Seattle

Manson

37

Lake Chelan State Park

Chelan

N

0   3

971

97

To Entiat

MILES

TOUR
37

Entiat Mountains

LOCATION: East of Leavenworth. Wenatchee National Forest. Chelan County.

HIGHLIGHTS: The Entiat Mountains' high ridgeline roads provide fabulous views of the Cascade Range, particularly from the lookout on 5,814-foot Sugarloaf Peak.

DIFFICULTY: Easy, though rocky in places, on native-surface roads with blind curves and narrow segments.

TIME & DISTANCE: 3.5 hours; 42 miles.

MAPS: Wenatchee National Forest, North Half (G-J, 7-9). *Washington Road & Recreation Atlas*, p. 73 (A-E, 7-10).

INFORMATION: Wenatchee National Forest's Lake Wenatchee and Leavenworth ranger districts.

GETTING THERE: Take U.S. 2/97 to Cashmere, southeast of Leavenworth. From the highway, take North Division Street north to North Cashmere Road. Turn right onto North Cashmere, then left onto Nahahum Canyon Road (county road 109/forest road 7412). Set your odometer to 0.

REST STOPS: Sugarloaf Peak Lookout. There are a number of campgrounds in the vicinity of the trip's north end.

THE DRIVE: Nahahum Canyon Road winds through a pretty valley of meadows, pastures and wooded hills. At mile 4.9 the pavement ends, and the rather steep climb into the Entiat Mountains begins. At mile 6.2 is the junction with road 7415. Go left here, then left again, following 7415's serpentine and picturesque northwesterly branch. In a couple of miles you'll have views into the Wenatchee River Valley. Mile 9.4 will find you at the junction with road 7400. The well-graded southwestern leg, to the left, descends to Peshastin (11 miles). Turn right, following the sign for Sugar Loaf Lookout, and road 7400 will take you north and then southeast. At mile 12.3 you will reach road 5200. Make a hard left here onto 5200, drive up the steep hill and take in a spectacular view of the Cascades. Soon road 5200 crosses to the east side of the ridge you've been following and enters a vast burned zone. (Large wildfires blackened the region in 1970, 1994 and 2001.) At mile 15.7 turn left at a Y for a short detour to a mountaintop viewpoint. By mile 23 you should be at the junction with road 5800. Continue north on 5200. The roadbed improves considerably by mile 23.2, where Eagle Creek Road (7520) descends to Leavenworth. At about mile 27.5, amid countless burned trees, the lookout road (715) is on your right. It's less than a half mile to a parking area below the site, established in 1914. From here the route continues north, eventually following a shelf. When it bends to the south, you're descending to Leavenworth.

ENTIAT MOUNTAINS

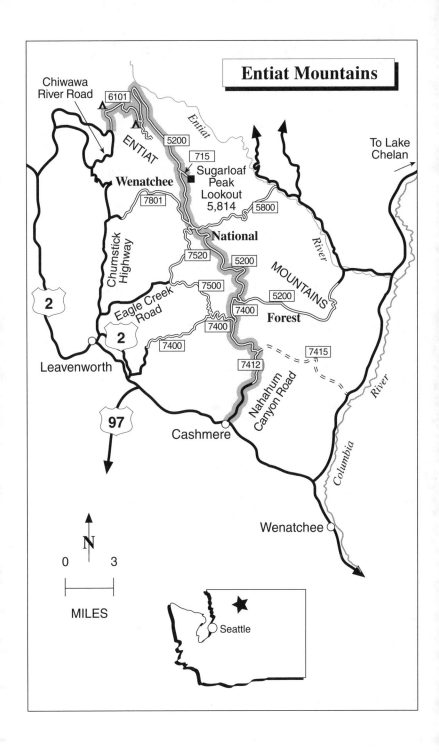

Entiat Mountains

Chiwawa
River Road

6101

Entiat

5200

715

Sugarloaf
Peak
Lookout
5,814

To Lake
Chelan

5800

Wenatchee

7801

National

Chumstick
Highway

7520

5200

River

MOUNTAINS

7500

7400

5200

2

Eagle Creek
Road

7400

Forest

2

7400

7400

7412

7415

Leavenworth

Nahahum
Canyon Road

7415

97

Cashmere

Columbia
River

N

Wenatchee

0   3

MILES

Seattle

105

Ruby Creek-Camas Creek

LOCATION: Wenatchee Mountains, west of Wenatchee. Wenatchee National Forest. Chelan County.

HIGHLIGHTS: With its high ridges and views of the craggy peaks of the Alpine Lakes Wilderness, and its deep canyons lush with many species of trees, this convenient (it begins and ends on U.S. 97) loop is a rewarding side trip from the highway.

DIFFICULTY: Easy, on roads that range from asphalt to narrow, high-clearance canyonside tracks with blind curves.

TIME & DISTANCE: 50 minutes; 14.7 miles.

MAPS: Wenatchee National Forest, South Half (G-H, 10). *Washington Road & Recreation Atlas*, p. 73 (E-F, 7-8).

INFORMATION: Wenatchee National Forest's Leavenworth Ranger District.

GETTING THERE: This loop begins and ends on U.S. 97, and you can take it from either end. **If you're southbound on U.S. 97:** About 5.3 miles south of the U.S. 97/U.S. 2 junction, turn left (southeast) at Camas Creek, onto forest road 7200. **If you're northbound on US 97:** About 2.1 miles north of the site of the bygone town of Blewett (milepost 174), once the booming hub of a 19th-century gold-mining district, turn right (southeast) at Ruby Creek, onto forest road 7204.

REST STOPS: There are no developed sites.

THE DRIVE: Road 7204, the more rudimentary yet intriguing southern leg of this loop, meanders along the deep trough of Ruby Creek, through a narrow, picturesque canyon that is wooded with a mix of deciduous trees and conifers. About 4 miles from the highway, after the route has joined road 140, it climbs to a high shelf, where you will have your first glimpse westward of the gray, angular peaks and ridges of Alpine Lakes Wilderness. Even better views lie a couple of miles farther on, at a summit roughly 3,600 feet high. When the road runs north and south, you're on road 7200. If you come up from the highway on road 7200, which is paved for about 3 miles, you will pass some large meadows dubbed Camas Land, dotted with stands of aspen. Beyond them the road bends south and twists, climbs and dips until it joins road 140, which will take you along the canyon of Ruby Creek and join road 7204, which in turn will take you to the highway.

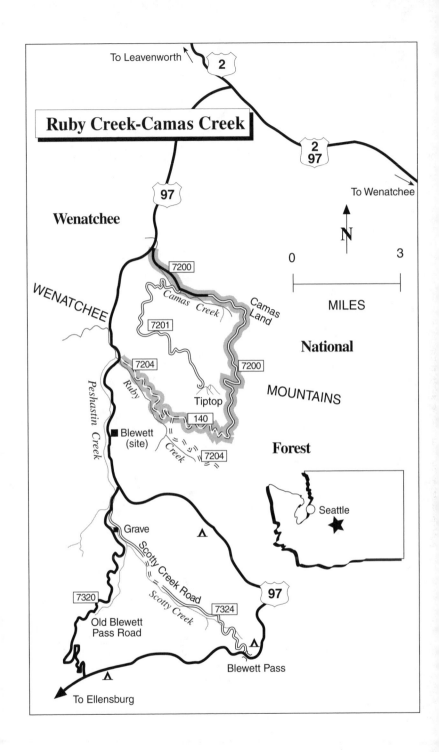

Ruby Creek-Camas Creek

To Leavenworth

To Wenatchee

97

Wenatchee

N

0   3

MILES

7200

Camas Creek

Camas Land

7201

National

7204

Ruby

7200

Tiptop

MOUNTAINS

Peshastin Creek

140

Blewett (site)

Creek

7204

Forest

Seattle

Grave

Scotty Creek Road

7320

Scotty Creek

7324

97

Old Blewett Pass Road

Blewett Pass

To Ellensburg

Scotty Creek

LOCATION: Wenatchee Mountains, southwest of Wenatchee. Wenatchee National Forest. Chelan County.

HIGHLIGHTS: For such a short side trip from U.S. 97, this little road through a once-bustling gold-mining district has much to offer, including a roadside grave dating from 1892, active placer claims and, of course, the road's pretty little namesake.

DIFFICULTY: Easy, on a good but narrow gravel road.

TIME & DISTANCE: 30 minutes; 7.8 miles beginning and ending at U.S. 97.

MAPS: Wenatchee National Forest, South Half (G-H, 10-11).

INFORMATION: Wenatchee National Forest's Leavenworth Ranger District.

GETTING THERE: To go north: Take U.S. 97 to Blewett Pass. Turn left (north) there onto forest road 7324. **To go south:** Driving south on U.S. 97, a little more than a mile south of the site of Blewett (milepost 174), the late 19th- and early 20th-century center of the area's gold-mining district, turn right (southwest) onto paved Old Blewett Pass Road (7324). Turn left in a mile, at Scotty Creek.

REST STOPS: There are no developed sites along Scotty Creek, but there are many appealing places to stop. There are two campgrounds nearby, along U.S. 97.

THE DRIVE: This is one of those little gems that modern-day motorists so often miss as they rush along the highways. Yet it's such a convenient, short and rewarding detour. If you find yourself on Blewett Pass, slow down and watch for the little gravel road that drops from the pass into the forest on the north side of the highway (which goes east-west on the pass). From the pass, it descends rapidly into the forest, and soon takes you along the edge of little Scotty Creek. If you're southbound toward the pass, pull off onto paved Old Blewett Pass Road west of the highway, and follow it a mile to Scotty Creek Road, on your left. Less than half a mile from the bottom of Scotty Creek Road, you'll see the neatly tended roadside grave of Pat King, said to be a freighter who died when he was 18 or 19. You'll see a number of posted placer claims along the creek, evidence that golden dreams still flourish in the drainage of Peshastin Creek, into which Scotty Creek flows. If you're heading west down from the pass, go right when you reach Old Blewett Pass Road to return to the highway.

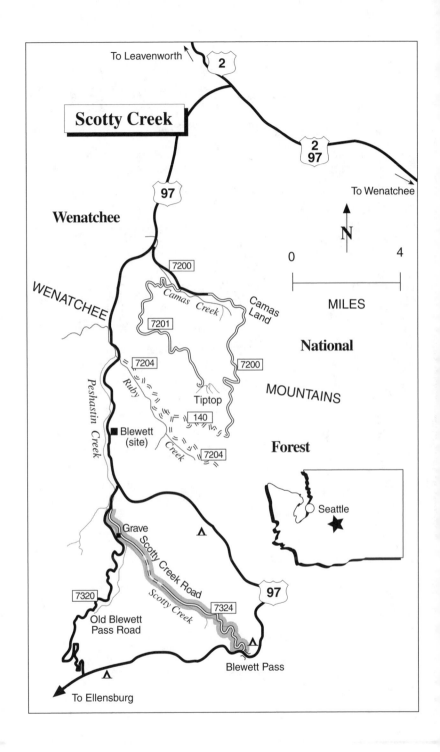

Scotty Creek

Roadside grave, Scotty Creek Road (Tour 39)

Cleman Mountain (Tour 46)

Carbon River Road

LOCATION: Northwestern corner of Mt. Rainier National Park.

HIGHLIGHTS: Carbon River Road, which parallels its name-sake waterway, passes through a rare inland, old-growth temperate rainforest of giant Sitka spruce, Douglas fir and western red cedar. It ends in the least-visited corner of the park, where visitors enjoy a rain-forest campground, and access to Carbon Glacier (which has the lowest-elevation terminus of any glacier in the Lower 48) and the famous 93-mile Wonderland loop trail around Mt. Rainier.

DIFFICULTY: Easy, on a good dirt-and-gravel road. But rainfall is heavier here than elsewhere in the park, and the road can be closed by flooding and washouts. Call ahead before going. Drive slowly on this narrow forest road, and turn on your headlights for safety.

TIME & DISTANCE: It's only about 4.8 miles from the park entrance to the campground and trailhead at road's end. But this is a remote corner of the park, and there is much to see and do. So it's best as a weekend destination at least. The popular Carbon River Trail is 7 miles (round-trip) from Ipsut Creek Campground to the Carbon Glacier overlook, with a 1,300-foot elevation gain.

MAPS: The park brochure is adequate. You can also refer to *Washington Road & Recreation Atlas*, pp. 84-85 (D-E, 6-7).

INFORMATION: Mt. Rainier National Park.

GETTING THERE: Take S.R. 165 south from Buckley toward the national park. About 3.5 miles beyond Carbonado, the road forks. The left branch goes to the park's Carbon River entrance (fee required) and Carbon River Road. The right fork goes to Mowich Lake (Tour 41). Set your odometer to 0 at the park entrance station.

REST STOPS: There is a picnic area midway along the drive. There's another at road's end, where there's also a year-round (depending on snow and road conditions) campground, Ipsut Creek. The campground has no potable water.

THE DRIVE: Few environments feel so mysterious, enchanting and full of life as old-growth forests, like the one that Carbon River Road passes through. The cedars and firs are of a size that only centuries of undisturbed growth can produce. The ferns are tall, the underbrush verdant, and the forest floor darkened by the high, dense, sun-blocking canopy of ancient trees. Take the time to observe the wide and rocky Carbon River, named for coal deposits found in the area. It is often swollen by rain and melt-water. In fact, the riverside road has been damaged by a series of floods, so be sure to check on whether it's open before coming to this remote corner of the park. (The road usually remains open to non-motorized travel regardless of motor-vehicle restrictions.) You're likely to encounter at least one spot where signs warn to check for flood damage before proceeding, evidence of the natural forces that prevail here.

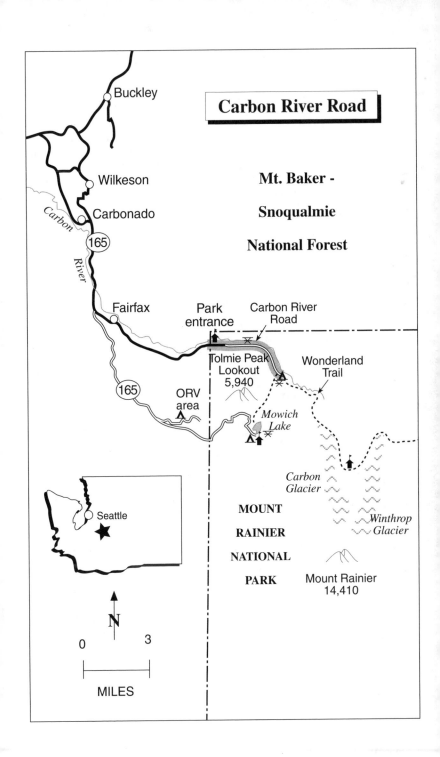

Carbon River Road

Mt. Baker -
Snoqualmie
National Forest

Buckley

Wilkeson

Carbonado

Carbon River

165

Fairfax

Park entrance

Carbon River Road

Tolmie Peak Lookout 5,940

Wonderland Trail

165

ORV area

Mowich Lake

Carbon Glacier

Winthrop Glacier

MOUNT

RAINIER

NATIONAL

PARK

Mount Rainier 14,410

Seattle

N

0   3

MILES

113

Mowich Lake

LOCATION: Northwestern corner of Mt. Rainier National Park.

HIGHLIGHTS: While the driving doesn't offer much adventure, you will encounter great views of Mt. Rainier and, at the end, a sparkling, almost 123-acre lake at 4,929 feet elevation, set in a glacial cirque surrounded by high ridges and verdant forest. Motor boats aren't allowed on the lake—named with a Chinook word for deer or animal—which helps to preserve the area's quiet, woodsy character.

DIFFICULTY: Easy. The first 3.2 miles are paved. The remainder is maintained gravel. The road is usually passable mid-July to October.

TIME & DISTANCE: 1 hour; 31 miles round-trip. But consider spending a full day or weekend enjoying this beautiful (and popular) lake and its nearby hiking trails.

MAPS: The park brochure is adequate. Or see *Washington Road & Recreation Atlas*, pp. 84-85 (D-E, 5-7).

INFORMATION: Mt. Rainier National Park. There is a ranger station at the lake.

GETTING THERE: Take S.R. 165 south from Buckley. About 3.5 miles beyond Carbonado, the highway forks. The left branch goes to the park's Carbon River entrance and becomes Carbon River Road (Tour 40). The right fork (still S.R. 165) continues to Mowich Lake (park fee required). Set your odometer there.

REST STOPS: There is a rather unappealing and exposed walk-in campground at the lake, as well as a picnic area. You will also find a small picnic area at the park's unstaffed fee station, not long after you enter the park.

THE DRIVE: The road to Mowich Lake provides fine views first of the long valley through which the Carbon River flows, then the deep trough drained by Voight Creek. Unfortunately, before you reach the national park, you'll have to endure the sight of clearcut mountainsides. The pavement ends 3.2 miles from the junction with the road to the Carbon River entrance. In another 7.7 miles you'll cross into the park. The fee station is 0.7 miles ahead. Once in the park, you'll no doubt find it refreshing to be in a more natural, protected and preserved environment, although this is a busy road, due to the popularity of the lake and the area's network of hiking trails. Among the latter is the 6.5-mile, 3-hour (round-trip) trek to 5,939-foot-high Tolmie Peak Lookout, built in 1933.

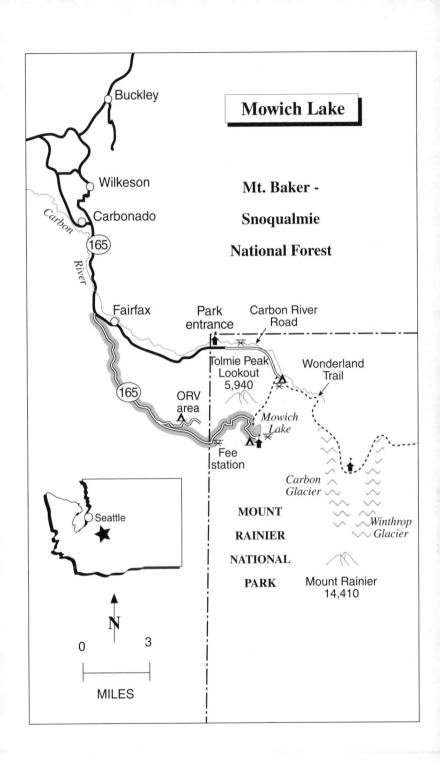

Mowich Lake

Mt. Baker -
Snoqualmie
National Forest

Buckley

Wilkeson

Carbonado

Carbon River

165

Fairfax

Park entrance

Carbon River Road

Tolmie Peak Lookout 5,940

Wonderland Trail

165

ORV area

Mowich Lake

Fee station

Seattle

Carbon Glacier

Winthrop Glacier

MOUNT

RAINIER

NATIONAL

PARK

Mount Rainier 14,410

N

0   3

MILES

Huckleberry Ridge

LOCATION: About 15 miles northeast of Mt. Rainier. Mt. Baker-Snoqualmie National Forest. Pierce County.

HIGHLIGHTS: Sun Top Lookout, built in 1932 on a 5,271-foot peak, provides an excellent view of Mt. Rainier, including Winthrop Glacier, and the Cascade Range—if the weather cooperates. The main road runs along Huckleberry Creek, passes a beautiful hiking trail into an old-growth forest, and then crosses high Huckleberry Ridge. There, from an elevation of more than 4,800 feet, you will have yet another view across a vast, tumultuous landscape of steep and deep canyons and seemingly endless mountain ranges.

DIFFICULTY: Easy, on graded gravel and native-surface roads. The hike is easy as well.

TIME & DISTANCE: 2.5-3 hours; 38 miles.

MAPS: Mt. Baker-Snoqualmie National Forest (E-F, 16). *Washington Road & Recreation Atlas*, p. 85 (C-D, 8-9).

INFORMATION: Mt. Baker-Snoqualmie National Forest's Snoqualmie Ranger District.

GETTING THERE: Take S.R. 410 toward The Dalles Campground, north of Mt. Rainier National Park's northwest corner. A mile north of the campground, or about 6.5 miles southeast of Greenwater, turn west onto road 73. Set your odometer to 0.

REST STOPS: There are tables at Sun Top Lookout. You can camp at The Dalles and Lonesome Lake campgrounds. There are many primitive campsites along the way as well.

THE DRIVE: Heading west on road 73, in 1.2 miles is the turnoff (road 7315, on the left) for Sun Top Lookout. It's a good gravel road, but you will encounter a gate in 5 miles that's open only on weekends (you can walk the remaining 1.1 miles to the lookout if it's closed). From that turnoff, you will cruise up a picturesque mountain valley. About 4.6 miles from the road to Sun Top the valley narrows, and you will reach a horseshoe bend where a small bridge spans Huckleberry Creek. You may see vehicles parked here, because it is the trailhead for a gorgeous hike along the creek, which cascades through a majestic old-growth forest. Follow the road through a gate and up the opposite wall of the valley, through a rockfall-prone area. The road narrows, and provides outstanding vistas as it takes you to the top of Huckleberry Ridge, down to Eleanor Creek and the park's northern boundary, and on to road 75, which you'll reach about 3.3 miles from Eleanor Creek. At the junction, you can go left (south) to the apparently overused campground at tiny Lonesome Lake, which has an artificial look to it. The trip goes right (north), snaking over Haller Pass to paved road 74 and, finally, White River and S.R. 410.

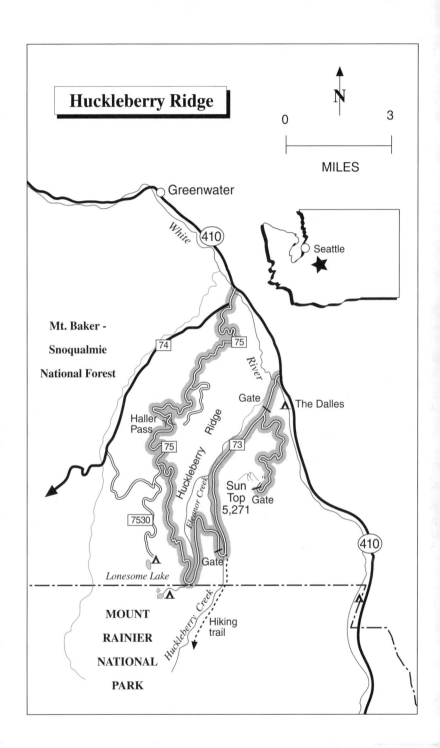

Quartz Mountain

LOCATION: Northwest of Ellensburg, Wenatchee National Forest. Kittitas County.

HIGHLIGHTS: The route follows South Fork Manastash Creek in a beautiful gorge, eventually bringing you to the pretty riparian area at Buck Meadows. The summit of Quartz Mountain (6,400 feet) provides a terrific view of deep valleys, the North Cascades and beyond. Road 4510, from Lookout Mountain over South Cle Elum Ridge, is narrow, serpentine, and quite exciting if you encounter a logging truck.

DIFFICULTY: Easy, on asphalt, gravel and dirt roads. Watch for ATVs, motorcycles and logging trucks. Turn on your headlights, and bring a CB radio to monitor the logging-truck traffic. You'll see the channel number they're using painted on roadside rocks.

TIME & DISTANCE: 3.5 hours; 70 miles.

MAPS: Wenatchee National Forest, South Half (D-G, 12-14). *Washington Road & Recreation Atlas*, pp. 86-87 (B-E, 3-8).

INFORMATION: Wenatchee National Forest's Naches and Cle Elum ranger districts.

GETTING THERE: From Canyon Road, at the southwestern edge of Ellensburg, zero your odometer and take Umtanum Road west and then south for 1.6 miles. Turn right (west) onto Manastash Road, at the old Dammon School.

REST STOPS: There are several campgrounds along the way, including a small, waterless one atop Quartz Mountain. There are also a few primitive vehicle sites and walk-in sites at Buck Meadows.

THE DRIVE: This rugged volcanic land has been deeply incised by streams that drain into the Naches and Yakima rivers from the high ridges, creating many scenic canyons to explore. The narrow canyon of South Fork Manastash Creek, with its high and steep rock walls, is particularly beautiful. The graded canyon road (31), though washboarded, is easy and very scenic. About 19.5 miles from Ellensburg you'll rise out of the canyon and enter the national forest. Several miles farther is the junction with road 3111, at wildlife-rich Buck Meadows, which is being restored after many decades of heavy human use. Stroll along the stream, then continue northwest (left at the junction) on road 3100 for 8 miles, to the spectacular summit of Quartz Mountain. (Take note of the junction with road 3120, which you'll take later.) Backtrack about 6 miles to road 3120, and turn left (northeast). In about 4 miles turn north onto road 3330 at Gnat Flat, and drive to Taneum Road (33), at Taneum Creek. You can return to Ellensburg (20 miles) by going right (east) on Taneum Road. Or for more driving adventure, go left (west) and follow road 3300 for about 11 miles. Then turn right (north), cross North Fork Taneum Creek, and follow the narrow, winding road (Woods & Steele Road) over South Cle Elum Ridge. (Watch for places to pull over if you encounter a truck.) In 8.2 miles is paved Westside Road. Cle Elum is 4.8 miles to the right.

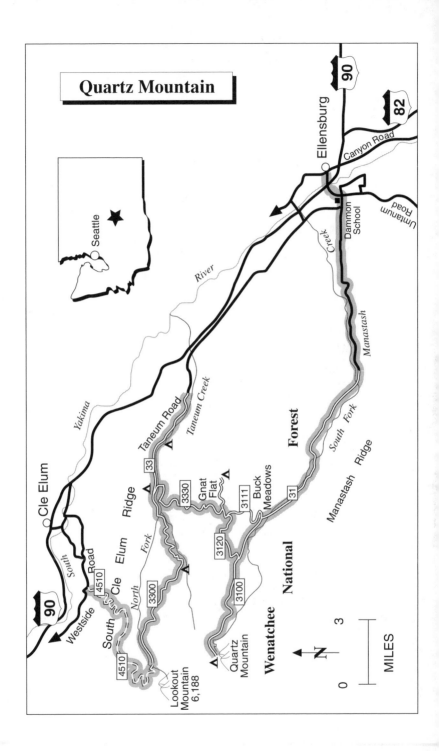

Umtanum Road

LOCATION: Southwest of Ellensburg. Kittitas and Yakima counties.

HIGHLIGHTS: This pretty country road, also called Wenas-Ellensburg Road, connects Kittitas and Wenas valleys via Ellensburg, passing through a checkerboard of private and state land. It meanders to Umtanum Creek, through the undulating hills, picturesque farmlands and rolling rangelands south of Manastash Ridge and north of Umtanum Ridge. It crosses Ellensburg Pass about midway. Early May, a beautiful time here, is also a fine time for birdwatching here.

DIFFICULTY: Easy, on a county-maintained road.

TIME & DISTANCE: 40 minutes; 18.5 miles.

MAPS: Wenatchee National Forest, South Half (F-H, 14). *Washington Road & Recreation Atlas*, pp. 86-87 (E-F, 6-8).

INFORMATION: Kittitas and Yakima counties.

GETTING THERE: This roughly east-west road can be taken in either direction. I think it's equally appealing either way. **To go west:** At the southwest edge of Ellensburg, at the junction of Umtanum Road (Damman Road on many maps), set your odometer to 0. Take Umtanum Road west and south. **To go east:** Take U.S. 12 to Naches, northwest of Yakima. Take Naches-Wenas Road northeast to Longmire Lane. Take Longmire Lane north to Wenas Road. Then take Wenas Road northwest to its end, at the junction with Umtanum, Maloy and Auduban roads. Set your odometer to 0 there.

REST STOPS: Umtanum Creek is a pleasant place to stop.

THE DRIVE: Going either east or west through the narrow vale drained by Umtanum Creek, fed by the streams that run down from Manastash and Umtanum ridges, you will climb gradually through hills of grass, sagebrush, aspen and pine. You may not even notice that the road is ascending some 1,500 feet to Ellensburg Pass. Along the way you will notice gray cliffs of volcanic rock, clear evidence of the landscape's molten origins. At the east end, the road emerges from the hills into the bustle of Ellensburg. At the west end, in contrast, you will find yourself in pastoral Wenas Valley, at the north end of paved Wenas Road and the east end of the Rocky Prairie tour (45), which you can take west.

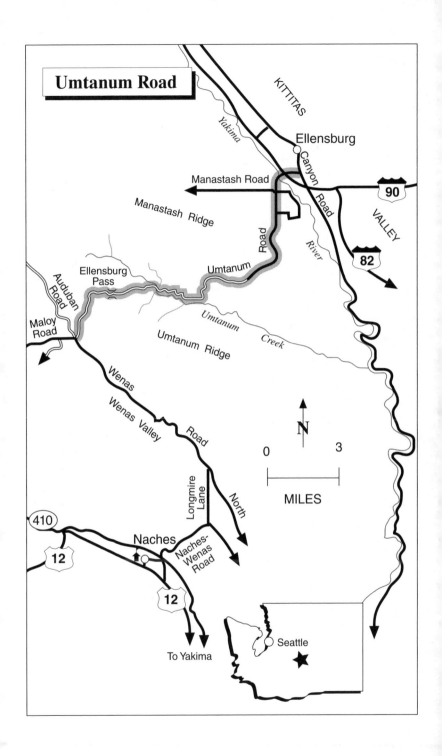

Umtanum Road

KITTITAS

Yakima

Ellensburg

Canyon Road

Manastash Road

Manastash Ridge

Road

River

90

VALLEY

82

Umtanum

Ellensburg Pass

Auduban Road

Maloy Road

Umtanum Creek

Umtanum Ridge

Wenas

Wenas Valley

Road

N

0   3

MILES

Longmire Lane

North

410

12

Naches

Naches-Wenas Road

12

To Yakima

Seattle

Rocky Prairie

LOCATION: Cleman Mountain, southwest of Ellensburg. Wenatchee National Forest and adjacent state land. Yakima County.

HIGHLIGHTS: Get ready for spectacular vistas across a deep river valley and rugged wilderness, as well as a beautiful and adventurous drive on a mild 4WD road amid several interesting canyons. This trip crosses Cleman Mountain, a high (almost 5,000 feet), 15-mile-long volcanic ridge named in 1868 for settler Augustan Cleman.

DIFFICULTY: It's easy on the west side of Cleman Mountain, on a narrow, maintained dirt-and-gravel road. I rate the east side moderate, since the native-surface roads are rougher and more rudimentary. The east side requires high clearance and, if you're heading west (uphill), four-wheel drive. Staying on course amid the east side's numerous spurs is the biggest challenge. Follow your map closely.

TIME & DISTANCE: An hour; 12 miles.

MAPS: Wenatchee National Forest, South Half (E-G, 14-15). *Washington Road & Recreation Atlas*, p. 86 (F, 4-6).

INFORMATION: Wenatchee National Forest's Naches Ranger District. Yakima County.

GETTING THERE: This east-west trip can be taken in either direction, as described under The Drive. **To go east** (the direction I recommend): Take S.R. 410 northwest for 13 miles from the junction with U.S. 12. Turn right (east) onto road 1701, Bald Mountain Road. Set your odometer to 0. **To go west** (which involves confusing junctions): Take U.S. 12 to Naches. Take Naches-Wenas Road to Longmire Lane. Take Longmire Lane to Wenas Road North. Take Wenas Road North to the junction of Umtanum, Maloy and Auduban roads. Set the odometer to 0, and take Maloy Road west.

REST STOPS: There are no developed sites.

THE DRIVE: Going east: From S.R. 410, Bald Mountain Road (1701) winds up the northeastern wall of Nile Valley, providing views to the west of the Naches River, Rimrock Lake and William O. Douglas Wilderness. In 3.8 miles you will be at a clearing, where a sign explains the volcanic origins and human history of the Manastash Ridge area. This is a junction of several roads. Keep right, go about 50 yards, and you'll reach a Y. The right branch, road 1712, is Tour 46 (Cleman Mountain). The left branch is road 1713, which you will follow past the meadow Rocky Prairie, and on down the east side of the mountain via a rocky two-track road with many spurs. As you descend toward Maloy and Wenas roads, watch for signs facing in the opposite direction, guiding westbound travelers to Rocky Prairie. When you reach Wenas Road North you can link up with Umtanum Road (Tour 44). **Going west:** On Maloy Road, you will come to a sign stating "End of County Road." Drive through a fence with a cattle guard, and the road will split; keep left. Soon you will pass a large steel

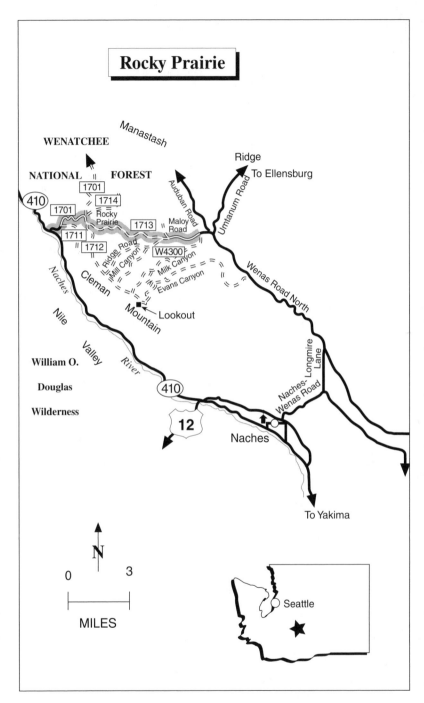

Rocky Prairie

Manastash

WENATCHEE

Ridge

To Ellensburg

NATIONAL FOREST

410

1701

1701

1714

Rocky
Prairie

1713

Maloy
Road

1711

W4300

1712

Ridge Road

Mill Canyon

Milk Canyon

Umtanum Road

Auduban Road

Wenas Road North

Evans Canyon

Cleman

Naches

Nile

Lookout

Mountain

Valley

River

William O.

Douglas

Wilderness

410

12

Naches-Wenas Road

Longmire Lane

Naches

To Yakima

N

0   3

MILES

Seattle

gate, on the left. That's road W4300, part of Tour 46, which climbs up Milk Canyon to the top of Cleman Mountain. Pass it, and 0.8 mile farther go through a gate. Where the road splits again; keep left. Stay to the right at the junction 0.2 mile beyond that (Ridge Road is on the left). Watch for signs directing you to Rocky Prairie. From there, continue to Naches Valley, or take Tour 46.

Cleman Mountain

LOCATION: Southwest of Ellensburg, at the eastern edge of the Columbia Basin. Wenatchee National Forest and adjacent state land. Yakima County.

HIGHLIGHTS: Cleman Mountain, a 15-mile-long ridge formed of Columbia Basin lava flows more than 10 million years ago, was named in 1868 for settler Augustan Cleman. It rises to an elevation of nearly 5,000 feet, some 3,000 feet above Naches and Nile valleys (to the west) and Wenas Valley (to the east). On a clear day it provides grand vistas from the forested Cascades, including Mt. Rainier and Mt. Adams, to the rolling, semiarid Columbia Basin.

DIFFICULTY: Easy, on roads that range from graded dirt and gravel to rough, loose rock. High ground clearance will be required.

TIME & DISTANCE: 1.5 hours; about 19 miles. But the extensive road network here provides more opportunities for exploring.

MAPS: Wenatchee National Forest, South Half (E-F, 14-15). *Washington Road & Recreation Atlas*, p. 86 (F-G, 5-6).

INFORMATION: Wenatchee National Forest's Naches Ranger District. Washington Department of Natural Resources.

GETTING THERE: Take S.R. 410 northwest for 13 miles from the junction with U.S. 12. Turn right (east) onto Bald Mountain Road (1701). Set your odometer to 0. Drive 3.8 miles to a four-way junction in an open area with a sign explaining the geologic and human history of the Manastash Ridge area (also see Tour 45, Rocky Prairie). Keeping right, drive another 50 yards or so, to a small Y. Road 1713 (Rocky Prairie) is the left branch. For this trip, take the right branch, road 1712, and reset your odometer to 0. My description begins here.

REST STOPS: There are no developed sites. Camping on the state land is not permitted.

THE DRIVE: For a couple of miles, the roadbed is rough, fractured rock, but you will be rewarded with a top-of-the-world vista as you climb toward a fire lookout (closed to the public). To the right (west), across the valley of the Naches River, lie the Norse Peak and William O. Douglas wildernesses, as well as Mt. Rainier. To the east lie the Wenas Valley, the Yakima River and Washington's vast agricultural lands. But if it's rainy and misty, you may not be able to see much of anything. At mile 4.6 is the top of Mill Canyon Road, on the left. Just beyond that is the state's Oak Creek Wildlife Area. About 1.3 miles farther, also on the left, is the scenic road down meandering Milk Canyon. (It's about 7.3 easy miles down to the junction with Wenas Road North and Umtanum Road, Tour 44, at the site of Wenas.) The lookout is less than a mile ahead. Just beyond it, Jones Road bends left and drops into Evans Canyon. About 1.4 miles from this turn, a two-track road branches left. Take it, and it will connect with Milk Canyon

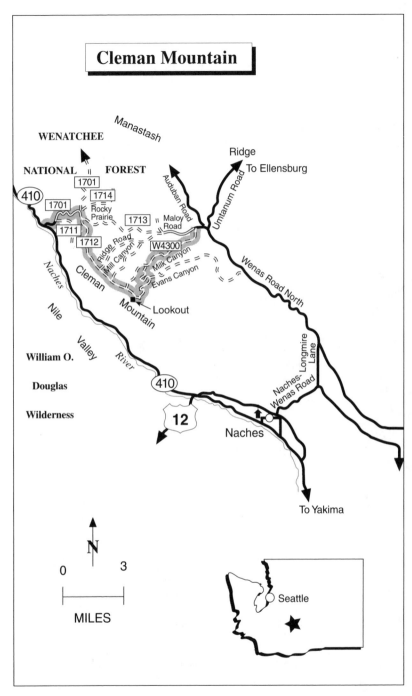

Cleman Mountain

WENATCHEE

Manastash

Ridge
To Ellensburg

NATIONAL   FOREST

410

1701
1714
Rocky Prairie
1713   Maloy Road
1711
1712
W4300

Auduban Road

Umtanum Road

Ridge Road
Mill Canyon
Milk Canyon
Evans Canyon

Wenas Road North

Cleman Mountain

Lookout

Naches

Nile

William O.

Douglas

Valley

Wilderness

River

410

12

Naches

Longmire Lane

Naches-Wenas Road

To Yakima

N

0   3

MILES

Seattle

Road (W4300) in 2 miles. Follow Milk Canyon Road down-canyon through the forest. In 3 miles is a junction, at a flat wooded area. Take the left branch. In 0.3 mile keep right at the fork, and a bit farther you'll reach a gate. Just beyond it is Maloy Road (1713). Go right, and take Maloy Road 1.8 miles to the junction of paved Wenas Road North and unpaved Umtanum Road.

Bethel Ridge Road

LOCATION: Between S.R. 410 and U.S. 12, northwest of Yakima. Wenatchee National Forest. Yakima County.

HIGHLIGHTS: Bethel Ridge Road climbs over a 5,000-foot-elevation volcanic ridge east of William O. Douglas Wilderness, passing through a mixed forest. The views of the valleys, ridges and peaks east of the Cascades are outstanding, as is the sight of the narrow, rock-walled canyon of Rattlesnake Creek, where anglers can cast for cutthroat and rainbow trout.

DIFFICULTY: Easy. The route is mostly gravel, with some asphalt.

TIME & DISTANCE: 2 hours; 33 miles.

MAPS: Wenatchee National Forest, South Half (C-E, 15-16). *Washington Road & Recreation Atlas*, pp. 86 (G-H, 3-4) and 100 (A, 3).

INFORMATION: Wenatchee National Forest's Naches Ranger District.

GETTING THERE: Take U.S. 12 to about 3 miles east of Rimrock Lake, or 17 miles southwest of S.R. 410. Turn north onto Bethel Ridge Road (1500) just west of Hause Creek Campground and the national forest information kiosk, and set your odometer to 0.

REST STOPS: There are developed campgrounds on U.S. 12, and you will see primitive campsites along the way. The view-point near the south end, and Timberwolf Mountain, are great places to stop.

THE DRIVE: The serpentine gravel road climbs steeply amid stands of ponderosa pine, providing ever-broader views of the long valley of the Tieton River and the high desert to the east. At mile 6.6 turn right (east) onto road 324, which zigzags across slopes of fractured rock to arrive at a stunning vista point in just over a mile. (More such views lie ahead on this road, if you want to explore it further.) Return to Bethel Ridge Road. On the north side of the ridge, it descends through more forest. About 3.5 miles from the junction with road 324, the road to Timberwolf Mountain (190) branches left (northwest), arriving in a couple of miles at a vista point from which you can see (if it's clear) Mt. Rainier and Mt. Adams. At the junction 6.2 miles farther, continue on road 1500 (now paved) toward S.R. 410. The road traverses a slope of still more shattered rock, and soon provides a vista of endless mountains, canyons and valleys as well as the steep-walled cleft through which Rattlesnake Creek passes. Eventually you will reach Nile Road, in the picturesque Nile Valley, the hamlet of Nile and S.R. 410.

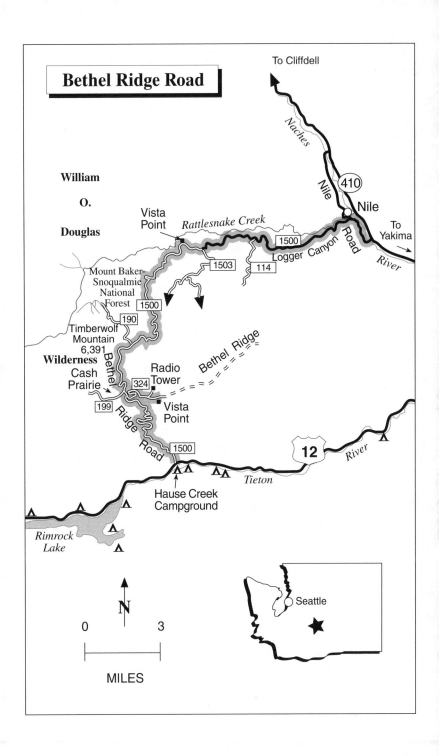

Bethel Ridge Road

To Cliffdell

Naches

410

Nile

To Yakima

William

O.

Douglas

Vista Point

Rattlesnake Creek

1500

Logger Canyon Road

River

Mount Baker-Snoqualmie National Forest

1503

114

1500

190

Timberwolf Mountain 6,391

Bethel Ridge

Wilderness

Cash Prairie

Radio Tower

Bethel

324

199

Vista Point

Ridge

Road

1500

12

River

Hause Creek Campground

Tieton

Rimrock Lake

N

0   3

MILES

Seattle

Colockum Road

LOCATION: Central Washington, northeast of Ellensburg. Kittitas County.

HIGHLIGHTS: In the 1880s, this mountain road over Colockum Pass (5,373 feet) was part of a long and important freight and emigrant route linking The Dalles, Oregon, the Ruby mines (Tour 29, Ruby Loop) and British Columbia, Canada. While I find the climb on the south side only moderately scenic, with a number of logged sites to look beyond, the northward descent offers inspiring vistas of the Columbia River, the North Cascades, and much of central Washington.

DIFFICULTY: Easy, although the roadbed is fairly rocky, especially on the north side of the pass.

TIME & DISTANCE: 2 hours; 30 miles.

MAPS: Wenatchee National Forest, South Half (K-M, 11-13). *Washington Road & Recreation Atlas*, pp. 73 (H, 12) & 87 (A-C, 10-12).

INFORMATION: Kittitas County.

GETTING THERE: From the south (the way I describe): Find your way toward Ellensburg. Northeast of Ellensburg, and north of Kittitas, take Brick Mill Road east to Colockum Road, which you will follow northeast over the pass. Set your odometer to 0 at Colockum Road. **From the north (Wenatchee):** Take Wenatchee Avenue/Malaga-Alcoa Highway southeast along the Columbia River. The highway will eventually become Colockum Road.

REST STOPS: There are many roadside places to stop (most of the land below the pass is privately owned). In the Colockum State Wildlife Area, camping is allowed within 100 feet of open roads unless posted otherwise.

THE DRIVE: Colockum Road, at the southeastern tip of the Wenatchee Mountains, becomes graveled in 2.2 miles as it climbs from Kittitas Valley into volcanic hills carpeted with sagebrush. But the sage is gradually replaced by meadows and stands of aspen and pine. About 14 miles from the start the road enters Colockum State Wildlife Area. At about the same point is the roadside site of Half-Way Station, in the 1880s a stop on what was then a well-used wagon road. A couple of miles farther, the canyon road that descends along Tarpiscan Creek to the Columbia branches right (it connects to Colockum Road down by the river). By now you'll be enjoying a vista across the pale vastness of central Washington, including the Columbia River. When you've descended from the pass you can continue to Wenatchee on Malaga-Alcoa Highway. But I suggest detouring left (west) onto little Kingsbury Road for a beautiful drive through Kingsbury Canyon. In 5 miles it will bring you to Moses Carr Road. Go right there, and make your way down to Malaga-Alcoa Highway.

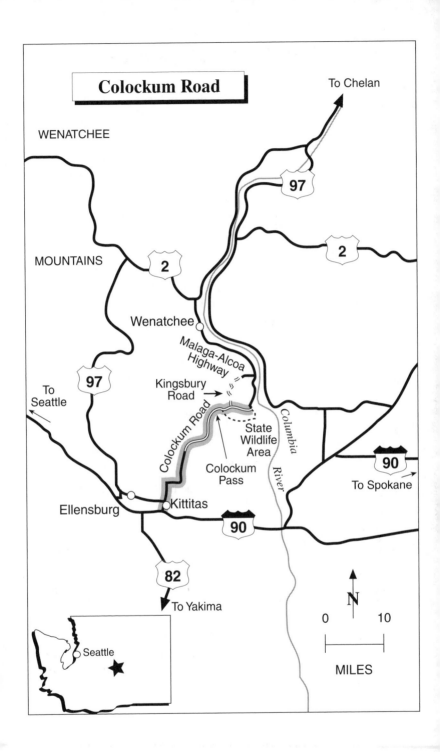

High Rock Lookout Loop

LOCATION: South of Mt. Rainier National Park's southwestern corner, in a southern part of Mt. Baker-Snoqualmie National Forest that is managed by Gifford Pinchot National Forest. Lewis County.

HIGHLIGHTS: The broad vistas (in clear weather) across the southern Cascades are outstanding. But the grand prize is the hike through old-growth forest to High Rock fire lookout. It is perched on the heart-stopping brink of a 1,200-foot cliff that provides an inspiring view of Mt. Rainier, just 13 miles to the northeast. You may also see Mount St. Helens, Mt. Adams, even Oregon's Mt. Hood. Be sure to bring a Northwest Forest Pass so you can park at the trailhead.

DIFFICULTY: Easy, on a road that includes asphalt, graded gravel and native dirt. The hike to the lookout, which gains almost 1,400 feet, is strenuous, and the weather is often cool and wet.

TIME & DISTANCE: An hour; 21 miles. Allow 1.5-2 hours more for the 3-mile (round-trip) hike to the lookout. The trail is usually clear of snow by July.

MAPS: Gifford Pinchot National Forest (E-G, 1-2). *Washington Road & Recreation Atlas*, pp. 84-85 (H, 5-7) & pp. 98-99 (A, 5-7).

INFORMATION: Gifford Pinchot National Forest's Cowlitz Ranger District.

GETTING THERE: Take S.R. 706 east toward Mt. Rainier's Nisqually entrance. About 2 miles east of Ashford, turn right (south) onto Kernahan Road East/forest road 52. Follow road 52 (open May to November) south and then east for 4.7 miles. Turn right (south) onto unpaved forest road 84. Set the odometer to 0.

REST STOPS: The lookout.

THE DRIVE: Considering how much logging has occurred in these parts, the drive along narrow road 84 is a surprisingly pretty one. At a Y at mile 6.8, where road 84 continues in a roughly southerly direction, keep climbing southwest on road 8440, toward Towhead Gap and the trail to 5,685-foot-high High Rock Lookout. At mile 9.4 the road reaches the gap, at the southern end of Sawtooth Ridge. You can park here and hike north on the ridge to the lookout (staffed in summer), an exhilarating locale that is not to be missed. From the gap, road 8440 bends north to the west side of the ridge, becomes narrower and rougher, and descends to Catt Creek. At about mile 14.4 you will reach paved road 85, which will return you to road 52.

ALSO TRY: Road 59, west of the park's Nisqually entrance and north of S.R. 706. It will take you 8.3 miles (one way) along the edge of Glacier View Wilderness, providing great views of Mt. Rainier before bringing you to Glacier View trailhead. From there, you can hike about 3 miles north to Glacier View Point, a former fire lookout site, for dramatic views of the active volcano and its glaciers.

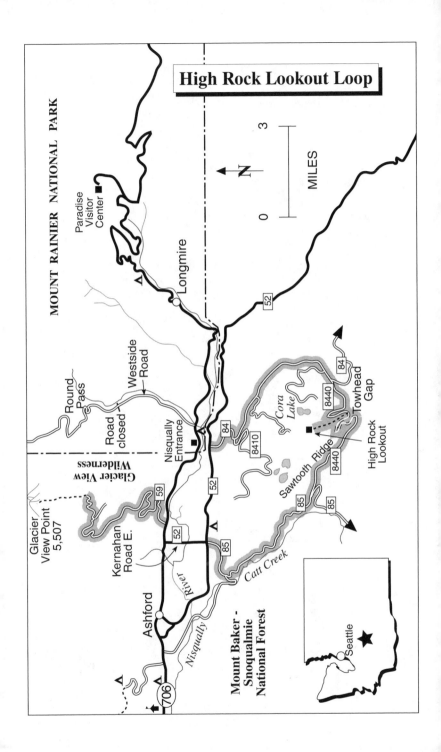

Mt. Rainier from Road 59 (Tour 49)

Mount St. Helens (Tour 52)

French Butte

LOCATION: South of Randle, northeast of Mount St. Helens. Gifford Pinchot National Forest. Lewis and Skamania counties.

HIGHLIGHTS: You will meander along the crest of a ridge that rises to an elevation of about 5,000 feet, providing spectacular views of Mt. Rainier, Mount St. Helens, Mt. Adams, even Oregon's Mt. Hood. The ridge is also a great place to pick huckleberries (peak season is mid-August to mid-September). Burley Mountain Lookout (5,304 feet) has a stunning view of the region. Built in 1934, it is one of only three functioning fire lookouts remaining in this national forest. Iron Creek Picnic Area is home to magnificent old-growth Douglas firs.

DIFFICULTY: Easy, on road surfaces that range from asphalt to gravel and dirt. Some segments are rocky, steep and narrow, with little room to pass and many blind curves. High clearance is required, and 4WD may be required as well. Almost 11 miles of the road at the north end are paved.

TIME & DISTANCE: 3.5 hours; 33 miles.

MAPS: Gifford Pinchot National Forest (F-G, 4-5). *Washington Road & Recreation Atlas*, pp. 98-99 (D-F, 5-6).

INFORMATION: G.P.N.F.'s Cowlitz Valley Ranger District. Ask for a map to areas that are good for picking huckleberries.

GETTING THERE: You can go north or south. **To go south** (the direction I describe): Take Hwy. 25 (Woods Creek Road) about 9.8 miles south from Randle, to Iron Creek Picnic Area. Turn into the picnic area, set the odometer to 0, and follow road 76 about 3.5 miles. Then turn right (south) onto road 77. **To go north:** From Hwy. 25 about 2.25 miles south of road 99 (to Mount St. Helens), turn east onto road 28. In 2.6 miles turn left (north) onto road 77.

REST STOPS: Iron Creek campground and picnic area.

THE DRIVE: Take a few minutes to admire the picnic area's old-growth Douglas firs, some of which have stood for 650 years. Then continue to road 77, which climbs through a beautiful forest, passing several small waterfalls. Almost 11 miles from Hwy. 25, asphalt gives way to gravel. At mile 13 you'll cross Greenhorn Creek, and 4.6 miles farther is a junction. Road 77 is to the right. For now, go left (north) on road 7605, toward Burley Mountain Lookout. When you reach another junction in 1.8 miles, keep right, and follow road 086, a narrow mountainside shelf, 0.6 mile to a locked gate and a parking area. From there, walk the road for a quarter mile or so to the lookout, which provides superb views of Rainier, St. Helens, Adams and Hood. Return to road 77 and continue south. Go straight through the four-way junction you'll soon reach, ignoring the gravel road that drops to the left and taking the little dirt road instead. As you climb, you will soon reach an open area that is thick with huckleberry bushes. As the road zigzags along the ridge, you will have alternating views of

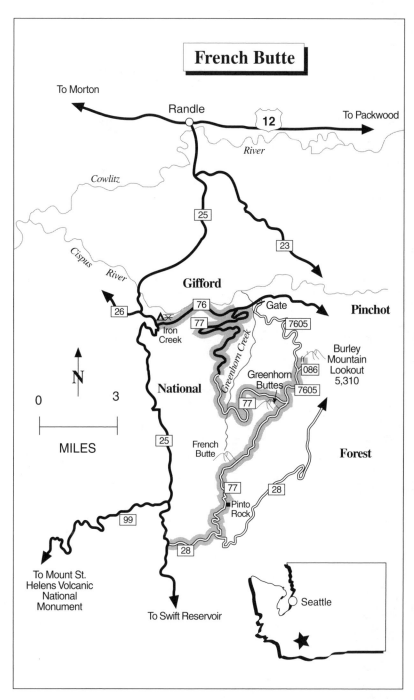

French Butte

To Morton

Randle

12 To Packwood

River

Cowlitz

25

23

Cispus River

Gifford

76

26

77

Gate

Pinchot

Iron Creek

7605

Burley Mountain Lookout 5,310

Greenhorn Creek

Greenhorn Buttes

086

N

0   3

7605

77

National

French Butte

Forest

25

77

28

Pinto Rock

MILES

99

28

To Mount St. Helens Volcanic National Monument

To Swift Reservoir

Seattle

Rainier and Adams. Continuing past French Butte, toward the promontory of Pinto Rock, you will suddenly be gazing at Mount St. Helens, which erupted in 1980. The road will pass below Pinto Rock, then descend to road 28, improving considerably. At road 28, go right (west), and you will reach Hwy. 25 in 2.6 miles.

Marble Mountain

LOCATION: Southeastern Washington, southeast of Mount St. Helens and north of Swift Reservoir. Gifford Pinchot National Forest. Skamania County.

HIGHLIGHTS: Outstanding views of two Cascade Range volcanoes: nearby Mount St. Helens, which erupted on May 18, 1980 with devastating force, and Mt. Adams, about 35 miles to the east.

DIFFICULTY: Easy, on roads that range from gravel to loose rock. High ground clearance and 4WD will be necessary toward the end. The turnaround spot at the end is tight.

TIME & DISTANCE: Less than an hour; 10.8 miles.

MAPS: Gifford Pinchot National Forest, (D-E, 6-7). *Washington Road & Recreation Atlas*, p. 110 (A, 4).

INFORMATION: Gifford Pinchot National Forest's Mount St. Helens National Volcanic Monument.

GETTING THERE: Drive to the west end of Swift Reservoir. There, take paved road 83 northeast to Marble Mountain Snow Park. Set your odometer to 0, and take the single-lane gravel road (8312) that branches off to the right (east) from the paved road.

REST STOPS: You won't need one on this short drive.

THE DRIVE: Road 8312 passes immediately through a gate, and heads directly toward a view of Mt. Adams, at 12,276 feet the second-highest peak in Washington and the third-highest in the Cascade Range. By mile 1.9 from the snow park, the haunting hulk of Mount St. Helens will present itself in all of its ominous glory. Views of the volcano continue as the road begins its meandering climb up the slopes of Marble Mountain. When you come to a four-way junction, continue directly ahead. After about 5 miles you can clearly see the course of the mud flows that roared down the valleys when St. Helens erupted, the force of which reduced its height from 9,677 feet to 8,363 feet. A short distance farther the road becomes considerably rougher, and you'll probably want to be in four-wheel drive. The road ends at mile 5.3. From here you can take a short walk to the summit (4,128 feet) for more great Cascade views.

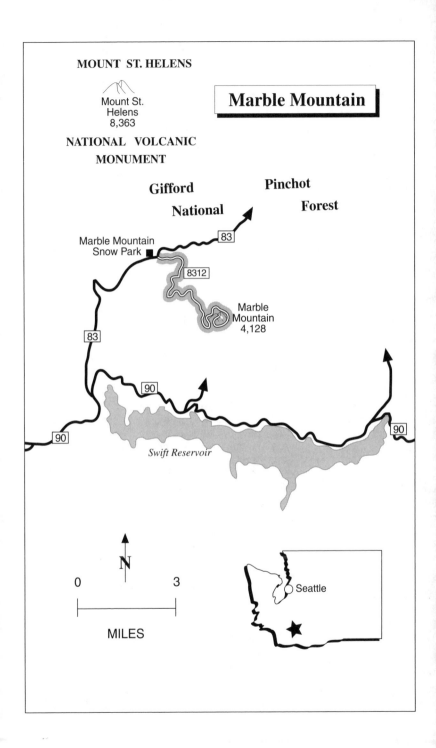

MOUNT ST. HELENS

Mount St.
Helens
8,363

Marble Mountain

NATIONAL VOLCANIC
MONUMENT

Gifford

Pinchot

National

Forest

Marble Mountain
Snow Park

83

8312

Marble
Mountain
4,128

83

90

90

90

Swift Reservoir

N

0   3

MILES

Seattle

Lookout Mountain

LOCATION: Cascade Range, 14 miles north of the Columbia River. Gifford Pinchot National Forest. Skamania County.

HIGHLIGHTS: You'll snicker at radio reports of traffic jams in Portland, Oregon, as you make the solitary climb from Sunset Campground to a beautiful ridge high above the East Fork of the Lewis River. The is a gorgeous drive, with shady forests, high ridges, deep valleys and broad vistas that take in Mount St. Helens, Mt. Adams and Oregon's Mt. Hood. The view from Lookout Mountain (4,222 feet) is not to be missed.

DIFFICULTY: Easy on the main route, which consists of gravel and native-surface roads. I rate the rough, rocky and narrow 4WD spur up Lookout Mountain moderate.

TIME & DISTANCE: 2 hours; 26.5 miles.

MAPS: Gifford Pinchot National Forest (C-F, 9). *Washington Road & Recreation Atlas*, p. 110 (E, 3-6).

INFORMATION: Gifford Pinchot National Forest's Mount St. Helens National Volcanic Monument, Mt. Adams Ranger District, Cowlitz Valley Ranger District, and Wind River Work & Information Center.

GETTING THERE: To go east from Yacolt (the way I describe): Take Railroad Avenue southeast to Northeast Sunset Falls Road (12). Take the latter east into Sunset Falls Campground and turn right, onto road 41. Set your odometer to 0 at the fee station. **To go west:** Take Wind River Highway (30) north from Carson to Stabler. Then take Hemlock Road west to the Wind River Work & Information Center and Hemlock Lake Recreation Area. Take road 43 west from there.

REST STOPS: Sunset Falls Campground, Lookout Mountain, Hemlock Lake Recreation Area (day use).

THE DRIVE: For the first 6.5 miles the single-lane road climbs through a picturesque forest, then emerges into the open to provide a grand vista across the steep valleys and countless mountain ranges to the west. At mile 8.5 the road reaches a ridgeline saddle with a fine view of Oregon's Mt. Hood. At mile 12.9 road 501, which climbs 1.1 miles to the summit of Lookout Mountain, is on the right (use low range 4WD). There's an electronics facility and the foundation of a bygone lookout at the top, where you'll find a world-class view of St. Helens, Adams, Hood, and the surrounding region. From the lookout turnoff, road 41 becomes more rudimentary, crosses a gap, then reaches the junction with road 4220. Keep right, continuing on road 41 for 1.3 miles to the junction with 43. Follow 43 on a long, steep descent into a piney forest, across Trout Creek and on to the Hemlock Lake Recreation Area, Stabler and Wind River Highway.

LOOKOUT MOUNTAIN

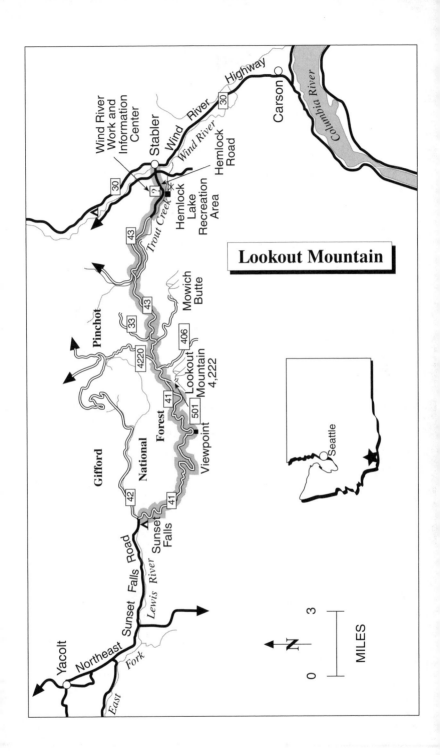

Lookout Mountain

Wind River Work and Information Center

Stabler

Wind River Highway

Carson

Columbia River

Wind River

Hemlock Road

Hemlock Lake Recreation Area

Trout Creek

Mowich Butte

Pinchot

Lookout Mountain 4,222

Viewpoint

Gifford

National

Forest

Sunset Falls

Lewis River

Sunset Falls Road

Northeast

East Fork

Yacolt

Seattle

N

MILES

0

3

139

Triangle Pass

LOCATION: Southwestern Washington, in the Southern Cascades northeast of Carson. Gifford Pinchot National Forest. Skamania County.

HIGHLIGHTS: Picture-postcard views across the Columbia River Gorge to the snowy cone of Oregon's Mt. Hood are the rewards of this pretty drive.

DIFFICULTY: Easy, on a good native-surface road. But watch for fallen rock in the roadway. There also are many blind curves on this serpentine road.

TIME & DISTANCE: 1.5 hours; 28 miles.

MAPS: Gifford Pinchot National Forest (G-H, 9). *Washington Road & Recreation Atlas*, p. 111 (E, 7-8).

INFORMATION: Gifford Pinchot National Forest's Mt. Adams Ranger District. Wind River Information Center, in Carson.

GETTING THERE: From Carson, on the Columbia River, take Wind River Road, a.k.a. Wind River Highway (30), north for about 3 miles. Turn right (east) onto Bear Creek Road (6808). Set your odometer to 0.

REST STOPS: There is a large pullout about midway on the drive that provides a terrific view of Mt. Hood. Panther Creek Campground, near the route's northern end, is very pleasant.

THE DRIVE: Bear Creek Road climbs steadily into the mountains north of the Columbia River Gorge, passing through stands of replanted timber. Looking south into Oregon, you will see the tip of Mt. Hood. Mile 12.7 will find you at Triangle Pass. Turn left there, onto road 68, and soon you will have a view across the river gorge. About a mile from the pass is a large pullout, where you can stop for a bit to gaze out at Mt. Hood. From here the road traverses grassy slopes, and narrows to a shelf. As you round a rock outcrop, slow down and watch for rocks in the roadway. Beyond that the road passes through the Wind River Experimental Forest, and a gate that is used to close the road to protect wildlife from Dec. 1 to April 1. A few miles farther, you will come to paved Panther Creek Road (road 65) and the end of the trip. Panther Creek Campground and Carson are to the left.

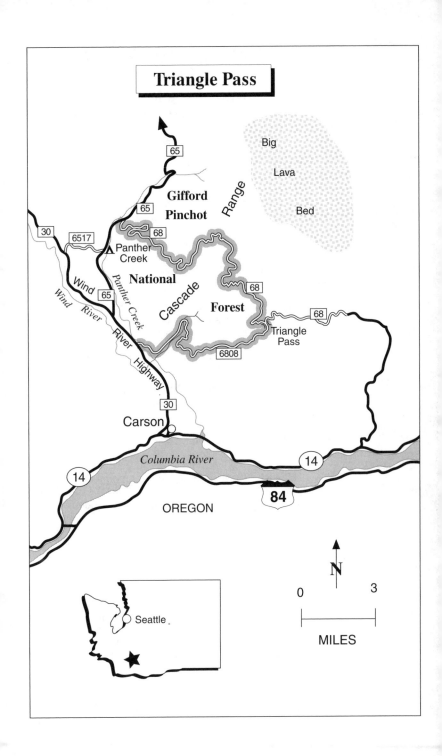

Triangle Pass

Big Lava Bed

65

Gifford Pinchot

65

68

30

6517

Panther Creek

National

Cascade

Range

Forest

68

68

65

Triangle Pass

Wind

Panther Creek

Wind River

River Highway

6808

30

Carson

Columbia River

14

14

84

OREGON

N

0   3

MILES

Seattle

Kendall Skyline Road

LOCATION: Blue Mountains east of Walla Walla, in Umatilla National Forest along the southwestern boundary of the Wenaha-Tucannon Wilderness. Columbia and Walla Walla counties, Washington; Umatilla and Wallowa counties, Oregon.

HIGHLIGHTS: Mile-high Kendall Skyline Road, built in 1928, is named for the U.S. Forest Service employee (William H. Kendall) who conceived, promoted and surveyed what remains one of Washington's most spectacular backcountry byways. It zig-zags for many miles along the crest of a narrow ridge that provides inspiring views of the rugged Wenaha-Tucannon Wilderness, Walla Walla Valley, canyons of Snake River country and Oregon's Wallowa Mountains. Don't pass up the spur to Table Rock Lookout (6,250 feet). Built in 1949, it provides an unsurpassed vista from southeastern Washington into Oregon and Idaho.

DIFFICULTY: Easy, on a native-surface road. But it's rocky and dusty much of the way. This trip is not for all-wheel-drive passenger cars. Snow can block the road well into July.

TIME & DISTANCE: 3.5 hours; 65 miles Dayton to Walla Walla.

MAPS: Umatilla National Forest, North Half (P-T, 2-4). *Washington Road & Recreation Atlas*, pp. 105 (F-G, 11-12) and 117 (A-B, 8-12).

INFORMATION: Umatilla National Forest's Walla Walla Ranger District.

GETTING THERE: From Dayton (the direction I describe): Turn southeast off Main Street onto South Fourth Street (which becomes North Fork Touchet River Road). Set your odometer to 0. Drive toward Bluewood Ski Area. **From Walla Walla:** Take Isaacs Avenue east to Mill Creek Road. Follow Mill Creek Road east and southeast to Umatilla National Forest, then take Tiger Canyon Road (65) on up to Kendall Skyline Road.

REST STOPS: Table Rock Lookout. Indian Campground.

THE DRIVE: From Dayton, follow North Fork Touchet River Road (county road 9115; No. 64 in the national forest) south, more or less, along its namesake into the steep, terraced and forested Blue Mountains. The pavement ends 13.8 miles from town, and 7.8 miles farther you'll pass the turnoff for Bluewood Ski Area. From that point the graded road diminishes to a more rudimentary single-lane mountain road. A couple of miles past the ski-area turnoff, the views down the region's many long, deep canyons become increasingly impressive. Beyond the turn for road 46 you will reach the crest of a ridge, where the serpentine road edges along the wilderness boundary. Soon you will reach a saddle with a terrific view of plains, canyons and summits. About 2 miles farther is the roadside monument to the man for whom the road is named. About a half mile farther is the turnoff for road 475, to Table Rock Lookout. In another couple of miles you will

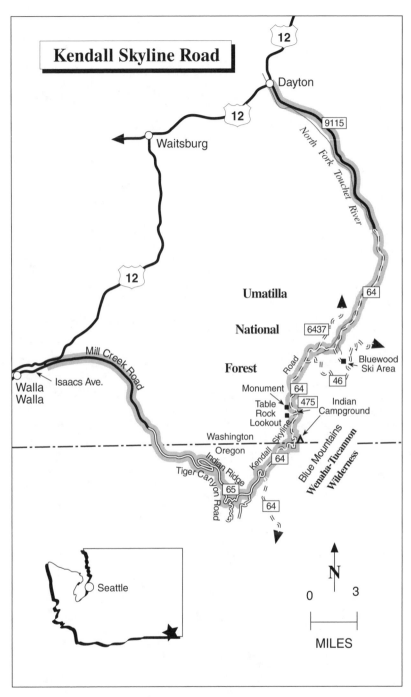

Kendall Skyline Road

pass Indian Campground and cross into Oregon. Several miles farther is the junction with road 65, a graded gravel road for the next 15.8 miles, when pavement resumes. Follow road 65 on a gorgeous descent back into Washington, and on to U.S. 12 and Walla Walla via Mill Creek Road.

Memorial on Kendall Skyline Road (Tour 54)

Joseph Creek Road (Tour 56)

West Mountain Road

LOCATION: Washington's southeastern corner, in the Blue Mountains west of Anatone, and along the eastern boundary of the Wenaha-Tucannon Wilderness. Umatilla National Forest. Asotin and Garfield counties. A segment at the southern end is in Oregon.

HIGHLIGHTS: Driving along narrow canyons and ridges that rise to an elevation of more than 6,000 feet will reward you with some of Washington's most inspiring vistas, which stretch from the Blue Mountains across incised Snake River benchlands to Oregon's Wallowa Mountains.

DIFFICULTY: Easy, although high ground clearance is necessary. Expect narrow sections with long drop-offs and little room to pass.

TIME & DISTANCE: 3 hours; 58 miles.

MAPS: Umatilla National Forest, North Half (W-Y, 2-4). *Washington Road & Recreation Atlas*, pp. 118-119 (A-B, 5-8).

INFORMATION: Umatilla National Forest's Pomeroy Ranger District.

GETTING THERE: Take S.R. 129 to Anatone, zero the odometer, and take Mill Road west for 1.8 miles. Keep left at the Y. Follow West Mountain Road (Mountain Road) into Umatilla National Forest.

REST STOPS: Camping is free at Wickiup and Misery Spring campgrounds, but neither has drinking water.

THE DRIVE: It doesn't take long to encounter the appeal of this drive: broad vistas across benchlands scored by the streams that flow into the Grande Ronde and Snake rivers. You'll enter the national forest about 7.5 miles from town, then pass the turnoff for Big Butte Lookout. But the views begin before that as West Mountain Road (4304) ascends more than 2,000 feet, onto a ridge between drainages to the north and south. About 14.5 miles from Anatone is the Wenatchee Guard Station, just one of many spots with first-class views. Continuing west, the road becomes No. 43, and brings you to the campground at Wickiup Spring. Here, road 44 branches off to the north, toward Asotin (27 miles). But continue on 43 toward Misery Spring Campground. Turn south (left) onto road 40, which follows a ridge that forms the eastern boundary of Wenaha-Tucannon Wilderness. The road becomes a mere shelf as it edges for several miles along the wall of a deep, steep and narrow canyon. It winds its way to Cabin Saddle, and on past a couple of roadside springs. Be prepared on this leg for a particularly narrow segment, with a heart-stopping drop-off, no room to pass, but a terrific view of a plunging canyon. Soon you'll see road 470, to Saddle Butte. Take it, and in 1.7 miles or so you'll be gazing out from a 5,900-foot flat-topped summit. Back on the main road (40), you'll descend into Oregon via switchbacks on the long, ear-popping descent on Grouse Flat Road (116) to the Grande

WEST MOUNTAIN ROAD

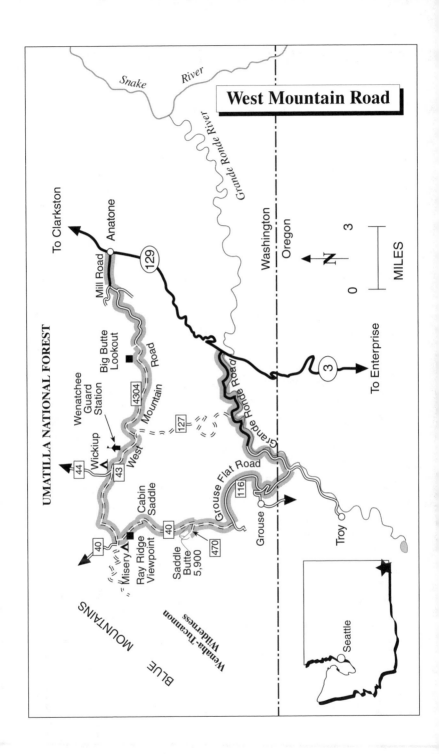

Ronde River, a federally designated wild-and-scenic river. Go left (east) at the river, and take winding Grande Ronde Road (100) through the river canyon, and back to Washington, asphalt and S.R. 129.

Snake River Road to Oregon

LOCATION: On the banks of the Snake River in Washington's far southeastern corner, and in the hills, canyons and benchlands west of the river. The southern segment crosses into Oregon at Hells Canyon National Recreation Area and Wallowa-Whitman National Forest.

HIGHLIGHTS: Although you won't travel into Hells Canyon, North America's deepest river gorge, you will be able to drive for miles between the terraced basalt walls along the river north of the gorge. Then you'll turn inland, and follow tributary canyons into the incised benchlands and furrowed hills west of Hells Canyon. Along the way is a short side to Red Hill fire lookout (5,020 feet).

DIFFICULTY: Easy, on roads that range from asphalt and maintained gravel to single-lane forest and rangeland roads.

TIME & DISTANCE: 3.5 hours; 92 miles.

MAPS: *Washington Road & Recreation Atlas*, pp. 107 (E-H, 10-11) & 119 (A-G, 8-11). Wallowa-Whitman National Forest, North Half (P-R, 1-4).

INFORMATION: Hells Canyon National Recreation Area. Wallowa-Whitman National Forest's Wallowa Valley Ranger District.

GETTING THERE: Take S.R 129 to Asotin. There, take either 1st Street or 3rd Street east about 0.8 mile. Turn south onto Wilson Street and continue to Snake River Road. Set your odometer to 0 there.

REST STOPS: There are toilets at Heller Bar, 22 miles south of Asotin. There are campgrounds toward the end of the drive as well.

THE DRIVE: The semiarid hills and volcanic cliffs that flank the Snake River (the boundary here between Washington and Idaho, and Oregon and Idaho) only hint at the great gorge farther south. But they are beautiful and impressive nonetheless, and contrast with the sub-alpine meadows, conifer-covered mountains and rainforests that one finds elsewhere in Washington. The pavement ends about 15 miles south of Asotin. Then you'll be on a two-lane gravel road all the way to Heller Bar, near the confluence of the Snake and Grande Ronde rivers. Continuing southwest, the road soon becomes Joseph Creek Road (after the famous Nez Perce Indian leader who is thought to have been born along it), No. 209. It diminishes, and bends away from the Snake, then crosses the Grande Ronde and climbs up the smaller, yet impressive, terraced canyon of Joseph Creek. You'll soon enter Oregon, where the road, now 699, bends east and, climbing steadily, enters H.C.N.R.A. Here the road is more primitive, and changes to Cold Spring Road (4680). It climbs to the crest of Cold Spring Ridge, which provides vistas across benchlands, canyons and rolling, golden hills. The roadbed improves considerably here, and occasionally edges close to the rim of Hells Canyon tributaries. Eventually you'll reach road 46, the southwestern boundary of

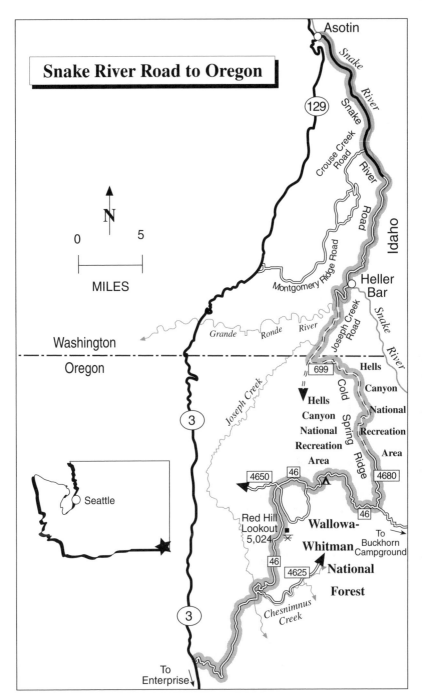

Snake River Road to Oregon

N

0 5

MILES

Washington

Oregon

Seattle

Asotin

Snake River

129

Snake River

Crouse Creek Road

Montgomery Ridge Road

Idaho

Heller Bar

Joseph Creek Road

Grande Ronde River

Snake River

699

Hells Canyon National Recreation Area

Joseph Creek

Hells Canyon National Recreation Area

Cold Spring Ridge

4650

46

4680

3

46

4680

46

Red Hill Lookout 5,024

Wallowa-Whitman

To Buckhorn Campground

46

Whitman

4625

National

Forest

Chesnimnus Creek

3

To Enterprise

H.C.N.R.A. To the left (southeast) is Buckhorn Campground, but go right (west), toward Enterprise. In less than 17 meandering miles you'll see Red Hill Lookout on the left. From there, road 46 descends amid rounded hills and narrow valleys to Chesnimnus Creek. Stay on road 46, and in about 15 miles you'll reach Oregon Hwy. 3.

APPENDIX

Information Sources

Colville National Forest
www.fs.fed.us/r6/colville

Republic Ranger District
180 North Jefferson
Republic, WA 99166
(509) 775-3305

Sullivan Lake Ranger District
12641 Sullivan Lake Road
Metaline Falls, WA 99153
(509) 446-7500

Three Rivers Ranger District
255 West 11th
Kettle Falls, WA 99141
(509) 738-7700

Gifford Pinchot National Forest
www.fs.fed.us/gpnf

Cowlitz Valley Ranger District
10024 US Highway 12
P.O. Box 670
Randle, WA 98377
(360) 497-1100

**Mount St. Helens
National Volcanic Monument**
42218 N.E. Yale Bridge Rd.
Amboy, WA 98601
(360) 247-3900

Mt. Adams Ranger District
2455 Hwy. 141
Trout Lake, WA 98650
(509) 395-3400

**Wind River Work &
Information Center**
1262 Hemlock Road
Carson, WA 98610
(509) 427-3200

**Hells Canyon National
Recreation Area**
www.fs.fed.us/r6/w-w/hcnra.htm
88401 Hwy. 82
Enterprise, OR 97828
(541) 426-4978
Clarkston, WA, **satellite office:**
(509) 758-0616

**Idaho Panhandle
National Forests**
www.nps.gov/ipnf
Priest River Ranger District
32203 Highway 57
Priest River, ID 83856-9612
**(On S.R. 57 about 3 miles
south of Nordman)**
(208) 443-2512

Kittitas County
Department of Public Works
411 N Ruby St., Suite 1
Ellensburg WA 98926
(509) 962-7523

**Long Beach Visitors
Information Bureau**
www.funbeach.com/
(**Also see:** Washington State
International Kite Festival,
www.kitefestival.com/)
Mail:
P.O. Box 562
Long Beach, WA 98631
In person:
Intersection of
Hwy. 101 and Hwy. 103
in Seaview
(800) 451-2542
(360) 642-2400

**Makah Cultural And
Research Center**
www.makah.com/museum.htm
Bayview Avenue
Highway 112
P.O. Box 160
Neah Bay, WA 98357
(360) 645 2711

**Mt. Baker-Snoqualmie
National Forest**
www.fs.fed.us/r6/mbs

Darrington Ranger District
1405 Emmens St.
Darrington, WA 98241
(360) 436-1155

**Glacier Public
Information Center**
(360) 599-2714

Mt. Baker Ranger District
810 Hwy. 20
(corner of Hwys. 9 & 20)
Sedro-Woolley, WA 98284
(360) 856-5700

Snoqualmie Ranger District
450 Roosevelt Ave. East
Enumclaw, WA 98022
(360) 825-6585

Verlot Public
Information Center
(360) 691-7791

Mt. Rainier National Park
www.nps.gov/mora/
Tahoma Woods, Star Route
Ashford, WA 98304-9751
(360) 569-2211, x. 3314

North Cascades
National Park
www.nps.gov/noca/
810 State Route 20
Sedro-Woolley WA
98284-1239
(360) 856-5700

Northwest Forest Pass
www.naturenw.org
(800) 270-7504

Okanogan County
Historical Society
www.omakchronicle.com/ochs/
P.O. Box 1129
Okanogan, WA 98840
(509) 422-4272

Okanogan County
Department of Public Works
1234 South 2nd Ave.
Box 232
Okanogan, WA 98840
(509) 422-7300

Okanogan National Forest
www.fs.fed.us/r6/oka/

Methow Valley Ranger District
24 West Chewuch Road
Winthrop, WA 98862
(509) 996-2266

Visitor Information Center
Building 49, Highway 20
Winthrop, WA 98862
(509) 996-4000

Olympic National Forest
www.fs.fed.us/r6/olympic/

Hood Canal Ranger District
North Quilcene Office
295142 Highway 101
P.O. Box 280
Quilcene, WA 98376
(360) 765-2200

Pacific Ranger District North
Forks Office
437 Tillicum Lane
Forks, WA 98331
(360) 374-6522

Olympic National Park
www.nps.gov/olym
600 East Park Ave.
Port Angeles, WA 98362-6798
(360) 565-3130

Outdoor Recreation
Information Center
(U.S. Forest Service &
National Park Service)
www.nps.gov/ccso/oric.htm
In the REI building at
222 Yale Avenue, North
Seattle, WA 98109
(206) 470-4060

Stevens County
Department of Public Works
185 E. Hawthorne
Colville, WA 99114
(509) 684-4548

Tread Lightly!, Inc
www. treadlightly.org
298 24th Street
Ogden, UT 84401
(800) 966-9900

U.S. Bureau of
Land Management
www.or.blm.gov/spokane/

Spokane District Office
1103 N. Fancher
Spokane, WA 99212-1275
(509) 536-1200

Wenatchee Resource Area
Wenatchee Field Office
915 N. Walla Walla
Wenatchee, WA 98801-1521
(509) 665-2100

Umatilla National Forest
www.fs.fed.us/r6/uma

Pomeroy Ranger District
71 West Main
Pomeroy, WA 99347
(509) 843-1891

Walla Walla Ranger District
1415 West Rose St.
Walla Walla, WA 99362
(509) 522-6290

Wallowa-Whitman
National Forest
www.fs.fed.us/r6/w-w/

Wallowa Valley Ranger District
88401 Hwy. 82
Enterprise, Oregon 97828
(541) 426-4978

Washington Department of
Fish and Wildlife
Sinlahekin Wildlife Area
www.wa.gov/wdfw/lands/r2snlhkn.htm
P.O. Box C
Loomis, WA 98827
(509) 223-3358

Washington Department of
Natural Resources
www.wa.gov/dnr/
P.O. Box 47001,
Olympia, WA 98504-7001
(360) 902-1004

Wenatchee National Forest
www.fs.fed.us/r6/wenatchee

Chelan Ranger District
428 W. Woodin Ave.
Chelan, WA 98816-9724
(509) 682-2576

Cle Elum Ranger District
803 West 2nd Street
Cle Elum, WA 98922
(509) 674-4411

Entiat Ranger District
2108 Entiat Way
P.O. Box 476
Entiat, WA 98822
(509) 784-1511

Lake Wenatchee Ranger District
22976 State Hwy. 207
Leavenworth, WA 98826
(509) 763-3103

Leavenworth Ranger District
600 Sherbourne
Leavenworth, WA 98826
(509) 548-6977

Naches Ranger District
10061 Highway 12
Naches, WA 98937
(509) 653-2205

Wilderness Press
www.wildernesspress.com
1200 5th St.
Berkeley, CA 94710
(800) 443-7227

Yakima County
Department of Public Works
www.co.yakima.wa.us/pubworks/
default.htm
128 N. 2nd St.
Yakima, WA 98901
(509) 574-2300

References

Alt, David D., and Hyndman, Donald W. 1984. *Roadside Geology of Washington.* Mountain Press Publishing Company.

Center of the American West, University of Colorado at Boulder. 1997. *Atlas of the New West: Portrait of a Changing Region.*

Benchmark Maps. 2000. *Washington Road & Recreation Atlas.*

Microsoft Encarta Encyclopedia 2000. Microsoft Corporation.

Northwest Interpretive Association. Road Trips: *Methow Valley Recreation Guide.*

Whitney, Stephen. 1989. *A Sierra Club Naturalist's Guide: The Pacific Northwest.* Sierra Club Books.

United States Department of Agriculture/U.S. Forest Service. Various national forest maps.

Index

Bold page numbers denote photographs.

Hoh River Trail, 36
Hood Canal, 32, 34, 35
Hood, Mt., 130, 134, 138, 140
Hooknose Mountain, 79
Hooknose Ridge, 78-79
Huckleberry Creek, 116
Huckleberry Ridge, 116-117
Hurricane Ridge, 24, 26
Hurricane Ridge Visitor Center, 24

I

Idaho, 86, 87
Idaho Panhandle National Forests, 86
Ione, 76, 77, 87

J

Jefferson County, 32, 36, 37
Jefferson, Thomas, 5
Johnson Creek, 100-101
Joseph Creek, 148, 149
Joseph Creek Road, **145**
Juan de Fuca Plate, 4
Junior Point, 97

K

Kaniksu National Forest, 77, 86, 87
Kelly Mountain, 66
Kendall Skyline Road, 142-143, **144**
Kendall, William H., 142
Kennewick, 10
Kettle Falls, 69, 73, 80, 81
Kettle River, 66, 67
Kettle River Range, 68, 69
King, Pat, 108
Kittitas, 129
Kittitas County, 118
Kittitas Valley, 121, 128
Kloochman Rock Trail, 36
Kloshe Nanitch, 30-31
Kloshe Nanitch Lookout, **29**

L

Lake Chelan State Park, 99, 101, 103
Leavenworth, 104, 105, 107, 109
Lewis County, 130, 134
Lewis, Meriwether, 4
locking differentials (lockers), 15
Lone Frank Pass, 50-51
Lonesome Lake, 116, 117
Long Beach, **xii**, 10
Long Beach Peninsula, 6, 40-41
Long Swamp, 50
Lookout Mountain, 118, 119, 138-139
Loomis, 50, 52, 53, 56, 57, 59
Loomis State Forest, 50, 52
Loup Loup Canyon, 89, 91

Loup Loup Pass, 89
Loup Loup Summit, 90, 91

M

Makah Cultural and Research Center, 20
Makah Indian Reservation, 20, 21
Makah Museum, 20
Makah Nation, 3
Makah Wilderness, 20
Manastash Ridge, 119, 121, 122, 123, 124, 125
Manhattan Project, 4
Manson, 102, 103
Marble Mountain, 136-137
Marble Mountain Snow Park, 137
Marblemount, 92, 93
Mazama, 44, 45, 48, 49
Metaline, 77, 78, 79, 83, 87
Metaline Falls, 77, 78, 79, 82, 83, 86, 87
Methow River, 44, 45, 48, 49
Methow Valley, 7, 45, 49, 60, 102, 103
Microsoft, 5
Middle Cascade Glacier, 93
Milk Canyon, 123, 124,125
Molson, 64-65
Molson Museum, 64
Molson School, 64
Monte Cristo, 94, 95
Mt. Angeles Road, 24
Mt. Baker Hiking Club, 42
Mt. Baker Ski Area, 42, 43
Mt. Baker Scenic Byway, 43
Mt. Baker-Snoqualmie National Forest, 42, 43, 44, 92, 93, 94, 95, 113, 115, 116, 117, 130, 131
Mt. Baker Vista, 43
Mt. Baker Wilderness, 42, 43
Mt Rainier National Park, 112, 113, 114, 115, 117, 130, 131, **132**
Mount St. Helens Volcanic National Monument, **133**, 135, 137, 138
Mountain Loop Highway, 94-95
Mountain Loop Scenic Byway, 95
Mowich Butte, 139
Mowich Lake, 113, 114-115
Mud Creek, 100-101
Mud Lake Valley, 65

N

Naches, 121, 123, 125
Naches River, 118, 123, 124, 125, 127
Naches Valley, 124
Nahahum Canyon Road, 104, 105
National Geographic/Trails Illustrated Maps, 9
Neah Bay, 20, 21
Neville Ridge, 89, 91

Wenatchee River Valley, 104
West Kettle River Road, 66, 67
West Mountain, 146
West Mountain Road, 146-147
West Snider Road, 31
Whatcom County, 42, 44, 48
White Chuck River, 95
White River, 117
Willapa Bay, 41
William O. Douglas Wilderness, 122, 123,
    124, 125, 126, 127
Winchester Mountain Lookout, 7, 42, 43
Wind River, 141
Wind River Information Center, 140
Wind River Work & Information Center,
    138
Winthrop, 44, 45, 48, 49, 60, 61
Winthrop Glacier, 113, 115, 116
Wonderland Trail, 113, 115

Y

Yacolt, 139
Yakama, 5
Yakima, 121, 123, 125, 126, 127, 129
Yakima County, 122, 124, 126
Yakima River, 118, 119, 121, 124
Yellow Aster Butte, 42

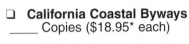

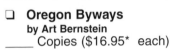
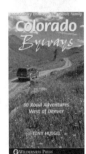
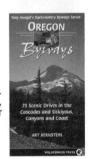

About the author

Tony Huegel is the author of a series of family-oriented guides for owners of sport-utility vehicles: *California Desert Byways, Sierra Nevada Byways, California Coastal Byways, Utah Byways, Colorado Byways, Washington Byways*, and *Idaho Byways*. He grew up in the San Francisco Bay Area, and is now an Idaho-based journalist.